Daily Grace

FOR MOMS
OF LITTLES

Endorsements

"IF YOU FEEL OVERLOOKED, ISOLATED, weary, and plain worn out as you are navigating mom-life, this book is for you. These pages are laced with encouragement and aim to help draw you closer to the source of strength: Jesus. Alexandra's raw, vulnerable stories are comforting and encouraging to those of us walking alongside her in the trenches of motherhood."

-Brianna Barrett

Writer, photographer, and mother

"EIGHTEEN YEARS AGO, I WAS a new mom. I had looked forward to that time of life when I could spend all day, every day, at home with my new little one. There were many things I needed during those mothering-of-littles years, but the one I'm most certain I needed the most was grace. *Daily Grace for Moms of Littles* speaks into those formative years of newborns, toddlers, and preschoolers—those years when we lack sleep, alone time in the bathroom, and grace for ourselves. Alexandra weaves a beautiful picture of God's truth through this devotional with Scripture, encouraging anecdotes, and soul-filling steps of faith. *Daily Grace For Moms of Littles* is a beautiful work that encourages every mom of littles to give themselves grace in the hard work of motherhood and to seek the never-ending grace of God daily."

-Nichole J. Swan

Founder of The Intentional Life Collective,
Author of *Numbering Our Days*, and mother

"*DAILY GRACE FOR MOMS OF Littles* is indeed for moms with young children; yet as a mom of six and three who are grown, I'd say this devotional is for all moms. Alex weaves a roadmap of hope, biblical wisdom, faithful steps, and prayer throughout the book. She elevates the role of motherhood and family life as the most God-ordained work we have. I will most definitely share this devotional with my friends."

-Sarah Green

Writer and mother

ALEXANDRA JENSEN

Daily Grace
FOR MOMS
OF LITTLES

50 DAYS OF KNOWING GOD MORE FULLY AND MOTHERING CONFIDENTLY FOR THE KING

Ambassador International
GREENVILLE, SOUTH CAROLINA & BELFAST, NORTHERN IRELAND

www.ambassador-international.com

Daily Grace for Moms of Littles
50 Days of Knowing God More Fully and Mothering Confidently for the King
©2025 by Alexandra Jensen
All rights reserved

ISBN: 978-1-64960-624-2, hardcover
ISBN: 978-1-64960-625-9, paperback
eISBN: 978-1-64960-674-7

Cover Design by Karen Slayne
Interior Typesetting by Dentelle Design
Edited by Emily Caseres

Unless otherwise indicated, all Scriptural quotations are taken from the Holy Bible, New International Version®, NIV® Copyright ©1973, 1978, 1984, 2011 by Biblica, Inc.® Used by permission. All rights reserved worldwide.

Scripture marked MSG taken from the The Message Copyright © 1993, 2002, 2018 by Eugene H. Peterson

Ambassador International titles may be purchased in bulk for education, business, fundraising, or sales promotional use. For information, please email sales@emeraldhouse.com.

AMBASSADOR INTERNATIONAL
Emerald House
411 University Ridge, Suite B14
Greenville, SC 29601
United States
www.ambassador-international.com

AMBASSADOR BOOKS
The Mount
2 Woodstock Link
Belfast, BT6 8DD
Northern Ireland, United Kingdom
www.ambassadormedia.co.uk

The colophon is a trademark of Ambassador, a Christian publishing company.

Dedication

YOU'VE PICKED UP THIS DEVOTIONAL for a reason! Maybe you are a mom-to-be, giddy with excitement. Maybe you are a brand-new mom, still in the infant stages of feeding and taking around-the-clock care of your baby. Maybe you have toddlers and are fighting to rise above the business and stay afloat. Maybe you have a child in kindergarten or early elementary school and are running on fumes transporting your children to and from all of the things. In whatever stage of mothering littles you are in, this book is for you. I pray the Holy Spirit will bless you in reading this book—that you will glean wisdom, gain insight, and establish your identity as a daughter of the King, a hand-picked mother whose only hope and holy help is found in Christ alone. Mama, this one's for you.

Contents

Introduction

WHAT DOES EVERY MOM I know (myself included) need? A daily dose of God's grace. God's grace softens our hearts. It makes us moldable and soft to Jesus' touch. God's grace sheds light onto our weaknesses in a constructive, loving way. God's grace builds us up and fills our cups. Mamas need grace like no other creatures on the planet. We are constantly running on empty, fighting to stay afloat. We are daily meeting the needs of everyone but ourselves. If there's anything we need (in addition to more coffee), it's God's lifesaving grace.

Mamas need grace. Grace is a mysteriously amazing, lifegiving, uplifting facet of Christ's holiness. But there is an even greater need that mothers possess. It is a deeper, more desperate cry of our hearts. The consolation to this most ravenous spiritual need is the truth. We need daily avenues of connection to Jesus. We need God's Word breathed into our lives like fresh oxygen to our souls. We need the Holy Spirit to descend onto our lives like a dove. We need the Holy Spirit's empowerment. We need the Bible's light-giving guidance. We need Jesus' living-water-infused wisdom. Grace has the unique ability to soften our hearts, but it is the truth that will ultimately set us free (John 8:31-32). God's truth enables us to not only survive as moms but also to thrive. Through God's life-giving Word, Christ's peace and joy can overpower our overwhelming circumstances.

I want you to enjoy this devotional. I most sincerely do! But first and foremost, I want you to explore God's Word for yourself. The Bible is alive and active, applicable to our lives today (Heb. 4:12). Read this devotional each day but also read a little slice of God's Word. (As a challenge, I encourage you to read the entire chapter of the daily Scripture provided.)

The Bible can illuminate our lives and change our hearts. The Bible can give us wisdom and daily connection to God's Holy Spirit. The Bible can enlighten our spirits and bring our souls to life like nothing else can.

The Bible can provide "a lamp for [your] feet" and "a light for [your] path" (Psalm 119:105) in an otherwise pitch-black world. Let God's Word be your light. Consider this devotional a reflection of its glory. But never trust the moon to accomplish what only the sun can do. The sun provides warmth, enables life, and catalyzes growth. The moon only reflects its glorious glow. Let God grow you through His holy Word.

Use this devotional as an additional resource in your daily walk with the Lord. Be encouraged in your motherhood journey. Tap into God's everlasting love and unfailing grace. God loves you dearly. His desire is for you. He wants your heart, soul, mind, and strength to be captivated by His holy presence. Rely on more of Jesus in your life to be transformed into a godly mom with a beautiful heart.

Remember, what you do, what you say, and how you say it is an outpouring of your heart. Purify the conditions of your heart by seeking the Holy Spirit to envelop you and fully encompass every chamber of your life. Leave nothing off limits. Go to God in prayer and tell Him everything. Do this often. Pray consistently. Keep the line of communication open between you and Jesus. God's grace flows freely through prayer.

We all execute unintended "mom fails" from time to time. In moments that feel like you've let the Lord down, depend on the Holy Spirit to illuminate your perspective, to shed light onto your circumstances, and draw you back into the grace of His warm embrace.

There is so much grace available to us because of what Jesus accomplished on the cross. The forgiveness, tender mercies, and freedom Jesus has for us knows no bounds. Abide by the well of God's grace. Teach your mind and train your heart to draw from it daily.

You've got this, Mama, for no other reason than because God's got you! You can be a grace-giving, community-building, seed-sowing, lie-destroying, love-lavishing, faith-fortifying, disciple-making, truth-proclaiming mother and daughter of the King through the strength, power, and might of Jesus alive in you.

The Greek word for "grace" is *charis*. It is linguistically and spiritually connected to two other Greek words: *eucharistia*, thanksgiving, and *chara*, joy. May this book be a place where you uncover and come to fully encompass God's grace through thanksgiving, which leads to glittering joy.

1
Consistency Is Key

"The kingdom of heaven is like treasure hidden in a field. When a man found it, he hid it again, and then in his joy went and sold all he had and bought that field. Again, the kingdom of heaven is like a merchant looking for fine pearls. When he found one of great value, he went away and sold everything he had and bought it."

Matthew 13:44-46

AN ARROW PIERCED MY HEART at bedtime when my little girl, Emma Claire, said, "Thank you, Mommy, for reading to me the Bible tonight!"

I read to her from her children's Bible, and things were seeming to click. She was asking questions and seemed to have some epiphany moments. What joy I could feel welling up inside of my mommy heart!

I don't write these things for you to think, *Good for her.* I write this to encourage you because hours prior, I was wiping poop off the bathroom walls; and hours prior to that I was yelling at my two-year-old son, "DO NOT EAT THAT WORM!" (He did not swallow it, but it definitely made it inside of his mouth.)

These are wild and crazy times filled with so much life and learning. My toddlers are like sponges, advancing in milestones and enhancing in knowledge by leaps and bounds daily. It is my job to weave the gospel message into their little hearts and minds at this crucial time in their developmental years.

As mothers in Christ, we impart Jesus into our children's lives through living by example, being vessels of the Holy Spirit through expressing love, joy, peace, patience, kindness, goodness, faithfulness, gentleness, and self-control (Gal. 5:22-23).

We make our children feel safe through consistent correction. When we discipline our children, we must be uniform in our approach. It makes our littles ones feel safe, confident, and secure when boundaries are developed through consistent discipline that is even-tempered and heartfelt. Every time I discipline my children, I try to give them a hug and tell them that I love them afterward. This sends the gospel message of Jesus. He loves us despite our sins and disobedience. He forgives us in full. Sometimes, we experience consequences from our sins and wrong choices, but the Lord disciplines us in a way that is just and consistent with God's heart and character. We must strive to love and correct our children in this same powerful way.

When we know and love Jesus for ourselves, teaching our children about him becomes more of a second nature. God's love overflows out of me and spills into my children's cups when I am connected with the Spirit of the Living God. We must become in tune and in touch with the heart of God, becoming mommies after God's own heart through God's Word and abiding in the Spirit daily.

The key is consistency. We must be consistent to demonstrate God's love, exude the fruits of the Spirit, discipline, disciple, and be in God's Word for ourselves. Through consistency, we engrain in our children's minds the message of what truly matters. Invest your time, talent, and treasure into the Lord's life-giving purposes.

Most days are roller coasters of whining, crying, time outs, kisses, hugs, laughter, tears, singing, and expressing big feels. These days have their hard moments; but they have some of the most rewarding, meaningful moments that teach me grace filled lessons along the way.

Jesus is refining me through motherhood. Allow your heart to soften to His touch so that Jesus can mold you like clay into the best mommy that you can be, all for God's glory.

Steps of Faith

- Pray this prayer. Let the words sink down deep into your spirit, and passionately plead for Jesus' presence to fill your heart to the brim:

  > *Dear Jesus,*
  >
  > *Pour out your Spirit and make me a vessel. Make my life an offering. As a mother, wife, and daughter of Christ, help me to become more like You and less like me. Help me to brilliantly reflect Your glory, goodness, and pure light. In moments that I fail, bring me back to the drawing board of Your plans, purposes, and desires for me. I want every piece and part of me—all of the components of my life—to radiantly reflect Your glory and light. In Jesus' merciful, mighty name, amen.*

- Think about a time when you felt most connected and in touch with God's grace. How can you be more intentional about living from the source of God's grace in your daily life?

2
A Sharpening Task

As iron sharpens iron, so one person sharpens another.

Proverbs 27:17

I AM GRATEFUL FOR THE little people in my life who sharpen me. They demand I set aside things that I am inclined to turn to and require I look upon their shining faces and give them my full attention instead. I am thankful for the little people God has planted before me. They grace my life and add so much laughter and light. I am grateful for the little people in my life who call me Mommy—so incredibly thankful.

Being a mom is challenging. This may be the understatement of the century. Let me rephrase: being a mom is an *Apollo* mission. It requires all of us—all of our heart, soul, and strength. I know that God designed motherhood to be this way. He created motherhood to turn us inside out. Motherhood requires us to yield our lives and forfeit some of our creature comforts for the betterment of our children. It requires us to lay down some of our blessings in order to bless the lives of our little ones. Motherhood wakes us from our bed of roses and demands we pick up our mats and travel beyond the borders of easy, quiet, and comfortable in our daily lives.

Being a mom is a selfless task. It requires us to step out of the spotlight and serve backstage. It requires us to push past our dreams and desires and help our little aspiring actors and actresses shoot for the stars. Will our own dreams and

7

life plans dissolve? No. But some seasons in life require us to look not only to our needs but also to the needs of others (Phil. 2:4). Motherhood is certainly one of these seasons; but according to the apostle Paul, we are to maintain this selfless mindset throughout the course of our entire lives. We must lend a hand when God calls us to aid and pursue the interests and God-dreams of others.

Your children are watching you. They are taking notes, no doubt. I want my children's notes to have scribbles of the cross and pictures of mommy holding Jesus' hand all over them. I want them to recognize the book that mommy reads every morning as the Word of God, the B-I-B-L-E. I want them to become confident, Christ-driven people who lead others to Jesus along the way. So I must model these godly attributes in my own life for my children to see. I must read my Bible and pray. I must lead my children to Jesus each day. I am so incredibly thankful for the role I get to play. Leading and feeding my children is a blessing. Children are a gift, a "heritage from the Lord" (Psalm 127:3).

Jesus wants all of me. He wants all of my heart, mind, soul, and strength to be fixated and focused on the gifts He has given me to further His Kingdom. Being a mom is certainly one of the most precious gifts He has given me, but I must be careful not to discount the fact that my identity is rooted in Christ alone.

Don't let motherhood become your idol. Serve the Lord in all things. Look to Jesus to fulfill your every need. Let your sense of self fall into the arms of Jesus. Be embraced by his tender love and care. Let His confident peace cover and carry you as a daughter of the King. Shoulder the cross of Christ throughout motherhood. Don't lose sight of the example you are setting, the impact you are making, and the eternities that are changing because of Jesus Christ in you. Keep in mind, your children are still watching, memorizing, and mimicking your moves, even when you are not wearing your "Mama cap." Represent Jesus well. Stand on Christ as the Solid Rock of your foundation. Continue to depend on Jesus for your daily bread.

I know that some moments of motherhood seem like tidal waves crashing; but depend on Christ's grace, compassion, and His God-instilled sense of joy to allow you to float. Let the current of the ultimate hope we have in Jesus carry you downstream, out of the storm. Jesus parts Red Seas in our lives and produces miracles in our hearts. When the disciples wondered who could enter the Kingdom of Heaven, "Jesus looked at them and said, 'With man this is impossible, but with God all things are possible'" (Matt. 19:26).

Draw sustenance from your Bible and through prayer. Motherhood was never meant to be easy; it is meant to make us more holy, to rid us of ourselves, and draw us closer to Christ's love and kindness. Lean in and rely on Jesus' strength when you feel depleted. Present to him your desperate need. Be thankful for the way he fills your cup. Seek him, and he will make his Living Water available to you—as He promised, "You will seek me and find me when you seek me with all your heart" (Jer. 29:13).

Are there happy moments? Certainly! But the ultimate purpose of motherhood is to draw us closer to the Lord by purifying our lives. In turn, Jesus unveils more of His heart. It is a beautiful, purpose-filled dance the Lord has ordained. Chase after Jesus and connect with God's heart, each day. It will make you a better mom and provide you with strength and wisdom along the way. Seek after and follow Jesus, and He will give you everything you need (Matt. 6:33). He wants to take you by the hand. Allow the Creator to intertwine His heart with your own.

Steps of Faith

- The next time the clouds well up and grace-filled tears fall from the sky, say a silent prayer thanking Jesus for the rain and the ultimate hope we have for a rainbow after our storms. Because of our salvation and the assurance of everlasting life through Christ Jesus our Lord, we can have confident peace and radiant hope through the ever-changing seasons of life. Let the rain be a tangible reminder of God's grace that falls freely on you.
- Write a letter to God expressing your gratitude for His grace.

3
Spirit-Woven Question

*"For God so loved the world that he gave his one and only Son,
that whoever believes in him shall not perish but have eternal life."*

John 3:16

MY LITTLE EM KEEPS ASKING me, "Is it Easter yet?"

Having just wrapped up Christmas, my response is quick and simple: "Not yet!"

I love that she loves Easter. I happen to be an Easter-lover myself. I admire the decorations and live for the fact that it is a celebration of God's love. It is my prayer that Emma Claire's love for Easter cultivates and grows as she comes to know, and unfolds for herself, the richness of its glorious meaning.

Christ made a way for us on the cross. He made a way for us to know Him and to love Him. He made a way for us to live for Him, equipping us with the power source of His Holy Spirit.

Jesus set an example for us. He came to answer our spirit-woven question, "Am I loved?" He came to console our hearts' desperate longing to be loved. He came so that we might know with confidence and certainty the answer to the inquiry, "What guarantees that I am forever and always loved?" The answer is, "Jesus. Jesus Christ, the Son of God." Those in Christ can live life in celebration of the fact that we have the hope of Heaven. Praise Jesus for Easter! Praise God for His redeeming love.

Love is a simple four-letter word. Everyone's imagery of love is a little different but relatively the same—a cake-topper bride and groom, his and hers towels, kisses and hugs—love! God's love offers a beautifully complex, deeply spiritual, knockout-punch powerful connotation. God's love is eternal. God's love is omnipotent and present in our lives today. God's love moves mountains and melts ice-encapsulated hearts. Christ's love enables us to live fully and to love others abundantly. His love inspires us toward generosity, courage, compassion, and good deeds. His love sets our captive, sinful souls forever free.

Because of the cross, we are free to live in love: to lavish grace and blessings upon others, to offer hope and light, to mother with all our might, and to live connected to the source of God's love through His Word. Love is a choice. It is a cognizant decision we must make each and every day. We must intentionally put on the character traits of Jesus Christ. We must wear coats of love, caps of salvation, and sneakers of peace. We must carry umbrellas of faith and have the pepper spray of God's Word with us at all times to ward off the enemies' attempts to rob us of what certain joy we are to encompass when we walk hand in hand with our Heavenly Father.

Easter is a celebration of God's love unfolding in our lives. Never stop living out the Easter message. Celebrate God's love and grace each day. Take strides of faith in knowing God more fully and loving others abundantly. Be intentional to pick out clothes that represent Christ's character. Put on the wardrobe of God's grace, love, readiness (which comes from the Word of God) and protection. Jesus wants to do a mountain-moving, mustard-seed-sprouting, amazing work in you as a mother and daughter of the King.

On this side of Heaven, there will always be a longing in our hearts to be totally and completely, fully loved. But because of Jesus, we have hope and can rejoice in God's love and faithfulness. Let every day be a celebration of the Easter miracle of Christ's resurrection. He is risen. He is for us. He is alive and active in our hearts today. *Rejoice!* The Lord is near (Phil. 4:4-5). Let your life be a reflection of Christ's resurrection story, an emblem of God's love.

Steps of Faith

- Pray this prayer:

  Dear Jesus,

  Thank You for the promise of John 3:16 in my life. May I always fall back on the truth that You love me beyond measure. Make my life as a mom a reflection of the gospel through love chosen during the hard moments and faith grasped through the struggle. In Jesus' risen name, amen.

- Reach out to another mother who you can connect with. Chat over coffee, tea, lunch, or on a walk and discuss the joys and challenges of motherhood.

- There once was a woman who was a relatively new believer, attending to her Bible study, giddy with excitement over a verse she had found in her Bible. As she began reading John 3:16 with complete awe and starstruck amazement out loud, tears streamed down the other ladies' faces. To them, the verse had become monotonous. But to the new believer, the verse was wondrous. We need to get back to that. Reread John 3:16, at the beginning of today's devotion, as if it were the very first time. Ask God to give you a new level of understanding and appreciation for this verse.

4
Worry-Free Mommy

David said to the Philistine, "You come against me with sword and spear and javelin, but I come against you in the name of the Lord Almighty, the God of the armies of Israel, whom you have defied . . . All those gathered here will know that it is not by sword or spear that the Lord saves; for the battle is the Lord's, and he will give all of you into our hands."

1 Samuel 17:45, 47

THE MOMENT I FELT SPIRITUALLY nudged to write about worry in motherhood, my palms began to sweat. I have always had a sweaty palms problem, but my palms soon became drenched. The truth is, when I try to brush off the fact that worry has at times threatened to envelop me, it seems to come back with a vengeance. So rather than cower in the corner, I choose to confront the giant of worry, fear, and anxiety head on.

The Bible says, "Do not be anxious about anything, but in every situation, by prayer and petition, with thanksgiving, present your requests to God. And the peace of God, which transcends all understanding will guard your hearts and your minds in Christ Jesus" (Phil. 4:6-7). The fact that God's Word talks about anxiety means that it is a real problem. As mothers, I fear that this problem is heightened because we have not only our own selves to worry about and take care of but also the very lives of the little ones we love and adore. We can state the words of Philippians 4:6-7 all day long; but if we do

13

not believe them and take steps to connect with the heart of God on this matter, then we have not unleashed the full potential of these fighting words.

Looking at how David confronted Goliath, we, too, can confront the giant of worry and anxiety in our lives. David's motives were not based on an earthly prize. In warding off worry, our motives need to be to align our hearts with the Lord's. David was not nearly as concerned about the prize of a wife and tax exemption that the king had to offer as he was about the fact that Goliath was directly defying God on Israel's soil. When we let Satan creep in and control our thoughts, we allow the enemy to defy the Lord God in His own temple. As temples of the Lord, where the Holy Spirit dwells, we are called and commanded to rise up and fight.

Fight against worry and anxiety in your life. Confess negative thought spirals to someone you know or love who cares about you. Be honest when someone in your life who wants to help you asks, "How are you doing?" Instead of brooding, start talking. The Lord equipped David. God equips us to fight off the enemy of worry and anxiety in our lives. "No weapon forged against [us] will prevail" with the Lord fighting for us (Isa. 54:17).

The following are tactical measures we can take to keep the enemy at bay:

- Rely on God's Word. It is available for you to read and glean wisdom from.
- Pray. Confess your worries and fears to God. Talk to Him out loud, in your car, while folding laundry, or scrubbing dishes.
- Memorize Scripture. This is a discipline we need to practice in our lives as avid believers and followers of Jesus. God's Word, written upon our hearts, is a powerful tool. It is a sword against which no other weapon stands a chance when wielded by the power and authority of the Holy Spirit in our lives.
- Call upon Jesus' name. Ask Christ to go before you, to rid you of all anxiety and fear.

Because we are held in the palms of God's hands, we are ultimately safe. The Lord's plans are for us. His plans are good. Fight against worry, fear, and anxiety in your life through God's Word, prayer, and carving Scripture into your heart that you can return to throughout the ever-changing seasons of life.

Steps of Faith

- Pray this prayer:

   Dear Jesus,

   Thank You for Your Word. Thank You that You are the Word (John 1:1, John 14:6)! You are the Living Truth, the ultimate Power and Authority to fight off fear, anxiety, and negative thoughts. Jesus, go before me and provide cloud cover to shelter me from the raging sun during my wilderness seasons. Help me to follow Your footprints in the sand. On cold, desert nights provide the fire of Your presence as a source of heat, light, and protection from the wolves that speak lies into my life. Protect me, God; equip me; and give me the strength to remain standing through it all. In Jesus' life-giving name, amen.

- David picked out five smooth stones to use to fight against Goliath. Pick out five verses that you want to memorize and have in the pouch of your shepherd's bag, written upon your heart. The following five verses are great options:

   - "Rejoice always, pray continually, give thanks in all circumstances; for this is God's will for you in Christ Jesus" (1 Thess. 5:16-18).
   - "I can do all this through him who gives me strength" (Phil. 4:13).
   - "Above all else, guard your heart, for everything you do flows from it" (Prov. 4:23).

- "And that is what some of you were. But you were washed, you were sanctified, you were justified in the name of the Lord Jesus Christ and by the Spirit of our God" (1 Cor. 6:11).
- "'Therefore do not worry about tomorrow, for tomorrow will worry about itself. Each day has enough trouble of its own'" (Matt. 6:34).

5
A Cheerful Heart

A cheerful heart is good medicine, but a crushed spirit dries up the bones.

Proverbs 17:22

I LOVE, LOVE, LOVE THIS verse—but unfortunately, we live in a spirit-crushing world. Bad things happen in motherhood and in life. We are living between two gardens—the garden of Eden and the garden that Jesus will establish when He returns. I look forward to this day. I am thankful for the fact that Jesus is coming back and will triumph over evil. I look forward to everlasting life in Heaven, eternal connection with my Lord and Savior. But in the here and now, we must work to maintain a mindset of sanctification, a heart of devotion, and a spirit of thanksgiving that brings hope and light to others.

Having a cheerful heart is a daily endeavor. We maintain a mindset of Christ through God's Word. Scripture is a force that is in motion, applicable to our lives today (Heb. 4:12). It can penetrate the lies that surround us and remove barriers to shed light onto God's truth of what is true, noble, right, pure, and lovely (Phil. 4:8).

Fight off negativity in your life through prayer, God's Word, and recognizing what you are grateful for. Only Jesus is able to alter the perspective of our circumstances. But through Christ, we can be "more than conquerors" (Rom. 8:37).

You are wholly and dearly loved (Col. 3:12). Through Jesus, we have the hope of Heaven someday. We must mother our children in light of this fact. God's Word changes everything. It can cause crushed-up, dry bones to come alive (Ezek. 37:10). It can empower a weary mother like me to dwell on the joyful components of even her most broken-down situations.

I've heard it said, "You steer where you stare." Look toward the light in your life. God's Word brings truth and goodness into our hearts and our homes. Invest your time in matters of eternity. Read God's love letter to us. Read, enjoy, and meditate on the Bible. It will change your life. It will alter the perspective of your circumstances. Read God's life-giving, holy Word. God's Word is like manna, a Heaven-sent portion of sustenance for our souls. In John 6:35, Jesus declares, "'I am the bread of life. Whoever comes to me will never go hungry, and whoever believes in me will never be thirsty.'" When we tuck God's Word into our hearts, we live abundant lives and are satisfied. We can live more grateful, cheerful, hope-filled lives as mothers when The Bread of Life is our daily portion.

Steps of Faith

- Pray this prayer:

  Dear Jesus,

  Help me to be faithful to get to know You more each day through my Bible. Give me diligence and persistence in this endeavor. Fill my heart in full when I seek You. Infuse my spirit with radiance and contagious joy. In Jesus' holy name, amen.

- Record today's Scripture, Proverbs 17:22, on a notecard. Place it somewhere within sight in your home.
- If you don't regularly read God's Word, I encourage you to do so. The Bible changes everything. It can enable your heart to thrive and provide water and light for a spirit of cheerfulness

and thanksgiving to flourish within you. Start by reading Psalm 100 today.

- Make a list or a note on your phone of five things you are thankful for. Revisit that list when your cup runs dry and you are feeling discouraged.

6
Release

When the dove returned to him in the evening, there in its beak was a freshly plucked olive leaf! Then Noah knew that the water had receded from the earth. He waited seven more days and sent the dove out again, but this time it did not return to him.

Genesis 8:11-12

WHEN NOAH OPENED THE WINDOW of the ark after the flood and released the dove, initially the dove returned empty-handed. It is easy to lose our sight when we are waiting for God's plans to unfold. We lose sight of God's promises. We lose sight of His past provisions. We lose sight of His enduring faithfulness. We lose sight, discount our hope, and abandon our confidence. But a week later, the dove returned with an olive leaf. A week after that, the dove did not return at all. She had found a tree, built a nest, and was being fruitful as the Lord ordained.

We must clutch our Bibles and cling tightly to our faith through the rainy seasons of life. The Lord is always willing to provide a rainbow, granted we ride out the storm. Even when our faith wavers, God's faithfulness never fails. It is an ark of safekeeping, something we can depend on and place our full hope in. Even when life presents itself as a piercing black night, we can have full confidence that the radiant rays of God's faithfulness are just beyond the horizon, ready to burst forth and penetrate the darkness. God's promises are as certain as the sunrise.

Sometimes, we lose sight of the fact that the Holy Spirit holds our children's hearts in the palm of His hand. We abandon our confidence in our little seeds. We lessen the value of our hope in their growth during the waiting seasons. We neglect ourselves the blessing of a spirit of light and joy when we are knee-deep in the wait. We throw our peace overboard and fixate on the problem. The truth of the matter is that sometimes the seeds we are planting in our children's hearts and lives are still in the process of coming to fruition. It's easy to become discouraged on tough days. But the key is diligence. Keep releasing that dove. Keep planting. It will be well worth it in the long run of your child's life.

Only God has authority and control over our children's hearts. Our job is to release the dove. Release the grip you hold on your child's heart and give it to the Lord. Faithfully disciple, love, forgive, and correct and let the Spirit of the Living God take care of the rest. Lavish Christ's love generously on your children. Be a cheerful, constant light in their lives. Pick up your watering can daily and grace their lives with the Living Water of Jesus in you.

The Lord is faithful. The Holy Spirit has the power to do anything. We need to pray for the Spirit of the Living God to impress on our children's hearts and minds. Let go of the seeds you so earnestly clutch and have faith. God alone has the power to create something beautiful and brand new from the dust. He makes beautiful things out of our children and out of us.

Steps of Faith

- Pray this prayer:

  Lord Jesus,

  I release my life to You. Have Your way in my home and in my heart. Help my children come to know and love You, in Your perfect timing. Help me to be a diligent seed-sower and trust

You with the rest. I have such great hope that You will complete the good work in my children's hearts that You've already begun. Give me wisdom to plant seeds in their spirits and wait on You for the rain. In Jesus' faithful name, amen.

- What dove do you need to release to the Lord? Is it an unanswered prayer? Is it the anticipation of the doctor's diagnosis? Is it a new job you have applied for? Is it the desire to do something meaningful, purposeful, and life-giving that spans beyond the realm of motherhood? Is it your children's hearts? We can release our doves through constant and consistent prayer. Prayerfully release the grip your heart holds over these things in the waiting period you are in. Allow yourself to experience joy and the love of Christ through this growing season.

- Meditate on the following Scripture: "Consider it pure joy, my brothers and sisters, whenever you face trials of many kinds, because you know that the testing of your faith produces perseverance. Let perseverance finish its work so that you may be mature and complete, not lacking anything" (James 1:2-4).

7
Where God's Provision Begins

Hear the word of the Lord, you Israelites, because the Lord has a charge to
bring against you who live in the land: "There is no faithfulness,
no love, no acknowledgment of God in the land."

Hosea 4:1

BABY SHOWERS, GENDER REVEALS, DELIVERY day preparation, matching mommy robe and infant swaddle, nursery decorating, parenting classes, doctor's appointments by the dozen—we've all been there! The beginning stages of motherhood are wistfully exciting. It's like the honeymoon phase of a relationship. Only in this case, let's call it the "babymoon" phase. The babymoon phase has its thrills and presents a future to look forward to when your bundle of joy arrives. You cannot wait to meet your little one; and when you finally do, your heart is full.

Days, months, weeks, and years pass by; and the spotlight moves off of you onto bigger, better, newer ventures of others. You feel a little lonely and somewhat forgotten. Sleepless nights, constant crying, dirty diapers, temper tantrums—reality sets in. You are a mom, a full-blown mom. And this is not a drill.

In the trenches, we need more encouragement than ever. We need the spotlight of God's presence shining down on us more than anything. We need godly influences surrounding our lives. We need biblical inspiration and godly truth breathed into us on a daily basis.

Although the babymoon phase was exciting, we can learn to be grateful for the season of motherhood we are currently in. We may be "in the thick of it," but God is right here with us. His presence envelopes our lives. His love, grace, and new morning mercies fill our mommy mugs in full. Where the babymoon phase ends is where God's provision begins.

The Israelites also experienced coming off a mountain high after being delivered from the Egyptians in the wilderness. At times, they complained, doubted God, and even worshiped other idols. Let us not fall prey to the same snares of the devil the Israelites became caught in. Let us learn from them and adopt hearts of gratitude and spirits of joy, acknowledging God in all we do.

We know that God is at work in our lives, even when the work is hard. We will experience hardships and daily struggles in motherhood, but God is with us. He is for us. His presence goes before us. His great love and stamp of approval is all that we need. Unlike the shifting spotlight and changing seasons of our lives, the Lord's zeal for our hearts remains ever-present.

Great is His faithfulness. Never-ending is His goodness. Everlasting is His love.

Steps of Faith

- Pray this prayer:

  Dear Jesus,

  Help me to live for You. May I strive to honor and please You above all else. Help me to remember that You are watching and notice me, even when no one else does. Help me to live for Your applause. In Jesus' worthy name, amen.

- In what small way can you praise the Lord today? Make a list and then give Him thanks!

- Read the following verses and remind Yourself that the Lord is Who You are living for: "A person is not a Jew who is one only outwardly, nor is circumcision merely outward and physical. No, a person is a Jew who is one inwardly; and circumcision is circumcision of the heart, by the Spirit, not by the written code. Such a person's praise is not from other people, but from God" (Rom. 2:28-29). How can you rely more on the Holy Spirit's daily provision in your life?

8
Mix Wisdom Into Your Life

Get wisdom, get understanding; do not forget my words or turn away from them. Do not forsake wisdom, and she will protect you; love her, and she will watch over you. The beginning of wisdom is this: Get wisdom. Though it costs all you have, get understanding. Cherish her, and she will exalt you; embrace her, and she will honor you. She will give you a garland to grace your head and present you with a glorious crown.

Proverbs 4:5-9

IT WAS EASTER DAY, AND my three-year-old daughter and I were making Funfetti cupcakes to celebrate Jesus' resurrection. Emma loves "helping" in the kitchen, and cupcakes seemed like an especially exciting feat. She pulled the barstool around the kitchen island to be front and center on the action (that is, right in the way). Pretending to be a mother who relishes having her toddlers "help" in the kitchen, I gave Emma her very own spatula for the endeavor.

"I mix myself!" she immediately insisted.

"Okay, baby, that's fine. But let Mama help you a little bit."

"I mix myself!" she hollered as she tried to pull the spatula, which was already dunked in cupcake batter, away from my helping grip.

"Okay, well, just lower your hand and keep the spatula in the bowl," I insisted to no avail. Her grip on the spatula was at the tail end of the handle, giving her little-to-no control over what she was doing.

"I keep my hand right here," she rebutted.

Batter began to go wild as Emma failed to keep her utensil in the bowl. I grabbed the spatula again to stop the snowball of what was quickly becoming a gargantuan mess.

"I do it myself!" Emma screamed, trying to jerk the spatula away from my helping hand with all her might. The more I tried to help, the more the situation escalated, until my daughter was a screaming banshee. "LET GO, MOMMY! LET GO OF MY MIXER!"

How often do we do the same thing with God? The Lord knows what is best for us as His children; He holds the plans of our lives in the palm of His hand. All He wants to do is to help and guide us; still, we insist on doing it our own way. "I do it myself!" we say. When we don't know the "why" behind God's corrections in our lives, we insist, "Let go of my mixer!" Instead of stopping, dropping our spatula, and bowing our heads to pray, we escalate the situation by continuing on in our defiant ways.

God wants what is best for us as His children. Sometimes, we fail to see the truth of this reality when we are caught up in the excitement and momentum of our lives. God wants to teach us the best way. He wants to show us how it's done. He doesn't want to ruin our fun, but He does want to direct us so that we are the best bakers that we can possibly be. The end product will be so much better, with much less of a mess to clean up in the end, when we let the head chef take His rightful place in our lives.

The wise heed the admonition of the Lord. Those with insight strive to follow the recipe of God's Word. Those with understanding seek after the ingredients that will lead to a righteous life. Those with wisdom are soft like dough, allowing the Lord to shape their hearts and lives, according to His will and way.

Jesus wants to train us to be fabulous sous chefs, but we must always remember our place is beneath the Head Chef, the Lord Jesus Christ. Let Jesus take hold of the spatula of your life. Do not bat away His helping hand. Mix the wisdom of the Lord into your daily life through God's Word, prayer, and fervently seeking the Lord's will in all things.

Steps of Faith

- The next time you enter your kitchen to prepare a meal, pray that the Lord would guide, direct, and go before you. In your culinary endeavors and in life, invite Jesus to be the Head Chef of your life so that He can teach you His ways of excellence and you will find success, favor, and the shield of God's love surrounding you in all that you do.

- Ask for the Lord's protection and direction over your life. Dwell on this verse: "Surely, Lord, you bless the righteous; you surround them with your favor as with a shield" (Psalm 5:12).

9
A Well-Built Home

As for everyone who comes to me and hears my words and puts them into
practice, I will show you what they are like. They are like a man building a
house, who dug down deep and laid the foundation on rock. When a flood came,
the torrent struck that house but could not shake it, because it was well built.

Luke 6:47-48

DO YOU KNOW HOW HARD it is to build a house? I honestly don't. But I can imagine the level of planning, hard work, and precision that takes place in order to assure that a house becomes a solid, aesthetically appealing structure. When we read God's Word and obey, we, too, are like a well-built home.

Home is a meaningful place. It's more than some latitude and longitude coordinates, more than a dot on a map. It's where much life and learning take place. It's where memories are tattooed, laughter cascades, and love unfolds.

Our relationship with the Lord should be like a well-built home. We lay a firm foundation through quality time spent with Jesus. We build structures of joy through nailing down hearts of gratitude and mindsets of praise. Is there grace when we fail to construct our lives in these ways? Yes! Christ's mercies are "new every morning" (Lam. 3:22-23). God is faithful, even when we are not. God's grace knows no bounds, but He honors our efforts to acknowledge His blessings. He delights in our longing to know Him more fully, to follow after Him more faithfully, and to understand His heart more intimately.

We must live more adamantly, persistently, consistently, and intentionally for Christ. This starts in our Bibles. The beginning of wisdom is knowing God (Prov. 9:10). By laying the foundation of our hearts on Jesus, through God's Word, we set ourselves up to know and grow in God's goodness. We can have peace from Jesus flowing through us because of God's life-giving Word. It is breathing and active, alive in our hearts, and applicable to our lives today (Heb. 4:12).

The Word of God will deconstruct you. It will tear you down only to build you back up again in a brand-new way. For us to be constructed in the best way possible, God has to be the builder. No carpenter other than Jesus will do. God's Word tears down the houses that we try to build for ourselves with our Styrofoam and hot glue guns. It constructs everlasting crystal mansions laced with sunflowers in their place.

The presence of the Living God ensures that we have the best materials, architectural plan, and builders possible. The Holy Spirit does all of the heavy lifting inside of us when we come before the Lord with heavy, humble hearts, looking to be unburdened, held close, seen fully, and loved completely.

Steps of Faith

- Pray this prayer:

> *Dear Jesus,*
>
> *Do construction work in my heart. Build up my life and fortify my mind through Your holy Word. Tear down the walls of sin and rid my heart of any blockades that I may have formed against You, unknowingly. Reveal to me the places and parts inside of me that need the Carpenter's touch. I am a sinner in need of a Savior. I commit my life to You and place the building plans in Your hands. Make my home and the conditions of my heart pleasing in your sight, oh Lord, my Rock, and my Redeemer. Amen.*

- Read the following words of Jesus: "Do not let your hearts be troubled. You believe in God; believe also in me. My Father's house has many rooms; if that were not so, would I have told you that I am going there to prepare a place for you? And if I go and prepare a place for you, I will come back and take you to be with me that you also may be where I am" (John 14:1-3). Close your eyes and imagine what Heaven will be like. State or write out a prayer thanking and praising God for preparing such a resplendent eternal home for you.
- Draw, paint a picture, or write a poem or a description of what you imagine Heaven to be like.

10
More Than a Mom

Many are the plans in a person's heart,
but it is the Lord's purpose that prevails.

Proverbs 19:21

DREAMS. EVERYONE HAS THEM—LITTLE SEEDLINGS God has planted and strategically placed, positioned to perfectly grace our hearts and the lives of others. These seedlings flourish and wither throughout the course of our days, changing along with the seasons of our experiences and life circumstances.

"Ready, set, grow," we say when we notice these seedlings taking root in our hearts, altering our mindsets in an eliciting way that connects us closer to the Creator. We are so eager to kickstart our relationships with the little seedlings inside of us that we deem ours to have and to hold that we begin to tighten our loving grip. Sometimes, we clutch our seedlings so fervently that no sunlight can penetrate through our tightly woven fingers. We love our seedlings so hard that we nearly smother them, stunting their growth.

At times, we love our seedlings more than the Creator Himself and fail in this way. Only when we release our grip and unleash our plant—our dreams and heart desires—from its prison can our seedlings flourish and grow. Our seedlings need the warmth and light that only our Heavenly Father can provide. God enables our seedlings to grow up and overflow out of our hearts, revealing His goodness, purpose, promises, and redeeming love in our lives when we choose to let go. We must "let go, and let God."[1]

Let God have His way in your heart and in your life. Even when the quilt of your life plans unfolds and reveals an image different than what you expected, look for the beauty and grace to be found in the perfectly imperfect stitches, patterns, and patchwork.

Nothing can stop God's plan for your life (Isa. 14:27). We may fight, squirm, and try to worm our way out of something that God has called us to; but ultimately, God will have His way. In the story of Jonah, we are shown that when God calls us to something, it is a command, not a recommendation. We are to listen and obey. Don't stay stuck inside the belly of a whale!

Something I tell my children often is, "Listen and obey, right away, with a happy heart!" Sometimes, I think I need this reminder for myself when it comes to my relationship with the Lord. When the Holy Spirit calls us to something, it is not really a suggestion; it is a calling: something with eternal purpose and everlasting value that has been positioned perfectly for us to accomplish.

Like David facing Goliath, Mary bearing the Son of God, Esther entering the king's court unannounced, and Mary of Bethany anointing Jesus by shattering an expensive bottle of perfume and pouring it out over Jesus' feet as an act of adoration, when we listen to God and obey, we, too, are performing an act of worship. We can praise Jesus and bring God glory through the way we live our lives. Through our steadfast obedience in carrying out the Lord's plans and purposes with a happy heart, we can be modern-day Davids, Esthers, and Marys.

The Lord equips those He calls. When God assigns a mission, He will give you all that you need to follow through. The strength, the courage, the wisdom, the accuracy, the provision—God will equip you with all of it.

---

1   Brianna Barrett, "Let Go and Let God," in *A Place of Grace for Moms of Littles* by Alexandra Jensen, Ambassador International, 2024, p. 153.

Our first job is to listen. We listen to God through His Word. We listen through prayer. We listen through Scripture spoken over us and wise counsel. In order to hear God's heart for us, we must come and sit at the feet of Jesus, with humble, willing hearts. Whisper, *"Anything, Jesus."* Lean in with open palms and an expectant heart and listen.

Our next job is to obey. We must obey the Lord in what He calls us to. I remember doing split leaps on the balance beam as a little girl. Jumping my highest and making my legs split as much as they could midair on the four-inch-wide beam was thrilling but frightening at the same time. I could do a partial split leap with ease and comfort, but giving it my all was a bit daunting.

A leap of faith can seem scary, but God trains us through muscle exercises and cardio that builds up our faith. He will never call you to something that you cannot accomplish (according to his artfully pieced, masterpiece-ordained way.) And when it seems like an impossible feat, He is going to spot you through it.

When you fall off the balance beam or the plans for your life readjust, then your "failure" was actually a learning experience meant to equip you, build resilience, and forge character—an imperative part of God's perfect plan. We need to redefine "failure," adopting a growth mindset that God's missions for our lives sometimes unfold in unexpected ways meant to fortify our faith.

We must obey right away. In gymnastics, the longer I waited to execute a certain skill, the more terrified I became in imagining all of the "what ifs." The best thing to do was to execute the skill immediately before hesitation set in. The same is true in our faith lives. We must do what God has called us to, right away.

We must obey with a happy heart. The Lord "loves a cheerful giver" (2 Cor. 9:7). Obeying God wholeheartedly is to be done with an attitude of gratitude and a mindset of pure joy. God has given you a specific assignment in furthering His Kingdom. This is something to be celebrated and faced with confidence. It's okay to feel the adrenaline kick in; but ultimately, we can have confidence that the Lord is going to aid us through all that He has called us to. At times, there will be redirection and moments that feel like failure; but ultimately, God is in control. The coach is spotting us with His righteous right hand that never fails, gives up, or runs out of strength to endure on our behalf.

We are more than moms. We are vessels of the Living God, created in advance for good works. When our hopes and dreams align with God's mission and we say yes to carrying out God's will in our lives, we are equipped with mountain-moving power because of our faith in Jesus.

Steps of Faith

- In motherhood and in life, the Lord gives us assignments to carry out for His Kingdom building purposes. Go to God in prayer. Ask Him what He has specifically called you to. Then pray this prayer of thankfulness:

  Dear Jesus,

  Thank You for equipping me for every good work in motherhood and in life. I pray that You would go before me and give me the courage to accomplish all that You have for me. In Jesus' righteous name, amen.

- Listen to God's answers throughout the day. Listen and obey when the Holy Spirit comes in and tugs on your heart. Listen and obey, right away, with a happy heart!

11
One Tough Gig

"I have told you these things, so that in me you may have peace.
In this world you will have trouble. But take heart! I have overcome the world."

John 16:33

MY FIVE-MONTH-OLD BABY'S CRYING COMMENCED and continued until it began to have a grating effect on my mental capacity. None of my attempts to soothe pacified or assuaged the crying. I was deeply troubled by the matter—that I could not help my baby. Through this mind-grating, heart-wrenching episode, I was reminded that God never said this would be easy; He said he would be with us always (Matt. 28:20).

Motherhood is one tough gig. One of the most assuring truths we have to rely on is that we serve one tough God! He literally had spikes driven through His hands and feet. A cat-o'-nine-tails was lashed across His back, many times. A thorny crown was crushed onto His head. When I begin to think this mom gig is too tough for me, I think of my Savior and realize it's not too tough for Him. "'[Christ's] power is made perfect in [my] weakness'" (2 Cor. 12:9). Praise the Lord, because I am so weak sometimes. When I depend on Jesus through this mom thing, His "'grace is sufficient for [me].'"

Sometimes, I feel ashamed to admit that motherhood is really hard. I put on this "Woman of Steel" mentality and attempt to fly and fight in my own strength until I hit a wall that becomes my kryptonite. One more dish, one more middle-of-the-night wake up call, one more meal to prepare, one more load of laundry to put away, one essential ingredient forgotten at the grocery store—some days, I fail. And when my rocket fuel propulsion runs out, I fall hard. Good thing Christ never fell off that cross. By choice, He remained hanging in pure agony, experiencing the worst kind of torture, until it was finished. Then He released His Spirit to God, and the veil was torn.

When things don't go according to plan, we must remain diligent as moms but with the practical realization that we are not superhuman. The Lord came and shed His blood so that we could experience freedom and peace, despite our sins, despite our shortcomings. Not all moments in motherhood are peaceful, but try to rely on the Lord as your daily bread. Through God's Word and prayer, we become equipped, Christ-driven mamas. Jesus' strength and grace are sufficient to cover and carry you through whatever the Lord has called you.

You have certainly been called and chosen as a mom—to mother your children with all your might, to discipline and disciple them according to God's Word—but not in your own strength. We must fully rely on God and not ourselves. We need His superpower force coursing through our veins. We need His mindset to shift our perspectives. We need His perseverance to carry us through. We need His strength and endurance in moments when we feel like we just can't. Take heart! Christ has overcome the world.

My baby soon fell asleep after drinking her bottle, and things immediately calmed down. The waves crashing in my mind settled. My frazzled sanity was straightened. It's almost as if Jesus said, "Be still," put my baby to rest, and calmed the sea in me. Jesus is always in full control of our circumstances, even when it feels like things have spiraled out of control.

In motherhood, there are many stressful moments and even some heart-punching experiences. Christ is with us through it all. We can have hope, even when the tempest sweeps in, because our God is with us (Isa. 41:10), "[He] is for us" (Rom. 8:31), He has already gone before us (Deut. 31:8). His "plans [are] to prosper . . . and not to harm [us]" (Jer. 29:11), for a joyful, grace-filled future. Whether on this side of earth or in Heaven, we will see the light and know His goodness.

There will be highs and lows in motherhood and life; but through it all, we can look for the light in knowing God's plans are *for* us. His purposes are good. We are enveloped in His grace. We are surrounded by His presence. We are held in His love.

Steps of Faith

- Close your eyes. Bow your head and soften your heart. Take one minute to breathe in and breathe out deeply, repeating this phrase like a prayer: (inhale) "Jesus Christ," (exhale) "Son of God," (inhale) "wash over me," (exhale) "for I am a sinner." Allow this prayer and breathing exercise to calm the crashing waves inside your heart. Reset your peace to be dependent on Jesus, not your circumstances.
- Peace is not the absence of chaos. It is found by seeking Christ's presence through the pandemonium. Meditate on the following Scriptures that pertain to the peace Christ provides through His holy presence:
  - "Let the peace of Christ rule in your hearts, since as members of one body you were called to peace. And be thankful" (Col. 3:15).
  - "Finally, brothers and sisters, whatever is true, whatever is noble, whatever is right, whatever is pure, whatever is lovely, whatever is admirable—if anything is excellent or praiseworthy—think about such things" (Phil. 4:8).
  - "You will keep in perfect peace those whose minds are steadfast, because they trust in you" (Isa. 26:3).

12
Testimony of Truth

"But seek first his kingdom and his righteousness,
and all these things will be given to you as well."

Matthew 6:33

I LOVE TO WRITE. IT is something that draws me closer to God's heart and pulls me into His presence like a warm embrace. It is the thing that holds me tightly and captivates my mind, heart, and attention. It is the way I raise my hallelujah. It does not have to be narrowed down to one specific thing, but what has the Lord called you to?

Motherhood is certainly a gift and a blessing, but what is it that fills your cup? Get into the Word. This is the thing that will make your heart tick. Whatever you like to do as an outpouring of your faith is an overflow of your connectivity to the Source. Jesus is the Source of life and truth. His words have an inspiring effect and impact on our daily lives. If you're not sure what "your thing" is, then I encourage you to get into the Word. Let God's Word and the Holy Spirit course through you and direct your paths. The Lord wants to take you to beautiful places and use you in a unique way for His Kingdom purposes. Plug in to the source of truth, hope, and life that we have through God's Word.

What is your testimony of truth? All because of Jesus, I am a wife and mother of three beautiful children. All because of Jesus, I write words that

I hope and pray will cause women's hearts to scoot a little bit closer to Jesus. All because of Jesus, I sell antiques and am able to make a little bit of extra income. All because of Jesus, I surrender my life each day and strive to lean in and listen to God's unfolding plans through the Holy Spirit. Your turn! All because of Jesus . . .

Be connected to the living source of God's Word and prayer. Let Jesus' guiding light lead you. As a believer, you have access to the Holy Spirit, but do you abide in the truth? *Abide* is a powerful word. Its connotation is "to continue without fading." May the Spirit of the Living God sparkle bright inside of you, every moment, every day as you abide in the beauty of His presence.

I truly believe that we can reach a deeper level of closeness with the Lord through immersing our minds daily in God's Word and seeking Jesus through prayer. I am not talking about the lighthearted, trivial kind of prayer. I am talking about deep, meaningful, expectant prayer. Praise God through prayer. Ask for the Lord's forgiveness through prayer. Present your requests to God through prayer. And do not forget to linger a little longer and wait to hear from the Holy Spirit through prayer.

Prayer is powerful. Prayer is effective. Prayer is like a golden thread that leads up into Heaven. It is a direct line of connection to our Lord and Savior. Depend on this thread to raise you up when life circumstances pull you down. Depend on this thread to lead you through darkness. Rejoice and praise the Lord when the slack line of prosperity and favor enables you to dance in green meadows near quiet streams (Psalm 23). Let the golden thread guide you along the path of God's righteousness and His plans for you. Depend on Jesus as your Lifeline through it all through prayer.

In all that the Lord has called you to, cling tightly to your Bible and remain steadfast in prayer. Let the things you do be a reflection of Christ, an overflow of how He is moving in your heart. Let the presence of the Holy Spirit guide you. Surrender your life to Jesus. Allow the everlasting cord of Christ's faithfulness and presence lead you.

Steps of Faith

- Pray this prayer:

  Dear Jesus,

  I praise You for instilling dreams and aspirations in my heart. Father, use me as a vessel. Utilize my strengths and weaknesses in unique and creative ways for Your Kingdom purposes. Employ me for Your plans. Show me how to shower the world with Your love and light in colorful ways. In Jesus' risen name, amen.

- Sweet sister, give yourself permission to dream. Release your inhibition and let the sheen of Jesus shimmer throughout your life. Never quench the spark of what God has lit inside of you! Follow the command of I Thessalonians 5:19: "Do not quench the Spirit."

13
Chin Up

My flesh and my heart may fail, but God is the strength of my heart and my portion forever.

Psalm 73:26

TAKE IT FROM A GIRL who's been there. Postpartum depression—check! Postpartum anxiety—check! Unfortunately, I have been there, trudged through all that muck.

Mama, I know what it is like. I have walked in your shoes. Being a mom is not applesauce and carrot sticks. Being a mom is not "cute" or easy. Being a mom is a lot of hard work with little-to-no credit. Being a mom requires us to lay down certain components of our lives to better serve our families.

By the grace of God, I have been pulled out of numerous pits in my mothering journey. I praise and thank God for His hand of protection over me and my family. I am grateful for doctors and counselors who have helped me along the way. If you are walking through a tough season as a mom, know that you are not alone.

According to the National Institute of Health, around one in seven women experience postpartum depression.[2] Other research findings show

---

2   UPMC, "Postpartum Depression: Causes, Risks, and Treatment at UPMC Magee-Womens in Central Pa." University of Pittsburg Schools of the Health Sciences, accessed August 24, 2024, https://www.upmc.com/services/south-central-pa/women/services/pregnancy-childbirth/new-moms/postpartum-depression/risks-treatment.

even higher statistics. Maybe this is not something you have experienced, but it is something to be aware of. We need to be on the lookout for other mamas in our lives, especially mamas with new babies. Bringing a new life into the world is a monumental, magnificent, massive endeavor and transition.

Maybe you have never struggled with depression, but your giants are Satan-silhouetted monsters all the same. Through it all, hold to the truth: the Lord is with you. God is for you. His presence envelops your life.

Paul recalled his own, very personal experience when the Lord allowed him to be inflicted with a thorn in his side: "But he said to me, 'My grace is sufficient for you, for my power is made perfect in weakness.' Therefore I will boast all the more gladly about my weaknesses, so that Christ's power may rest on me" (2 Cor. 12:9). Paul pleaded with the Lord to take the thorn from him; but for some reason, the Lord did not. His thorn caused him to lean in on the Lord Jesus Christ for daily strength and comfort. It made him depend on God's Word and prayer.

While biblical scholars remain unsure as to what this thorn was, it was some sort of impairment that affected Paul's day-to-day living. It could have been a sin struggle. It could have been a physical affliction. We're not sure. But whatever it was, it agonized him. It caused him much pain. So it is with our daily struggles, our weaknesses.

I love the hope the continuation of Paul's declaration has to offer: "*That is why, for Christ's sake, I delight* in weaknesses, in insults, in hardships, in persecutions, in difficulties. For when I am weak, then I am strong" (2 Cor. 12:10, emphasis mine). For the sake of Christ, we can learn to be content in every season. Whether rich or poor, desert or well-watered shores, peace or chaos, there is still joy to be found "for Christ's sake" in our lives. This is not a quick fix; but in time, with persistence, and intentionality, we can train our minds and hearts to look for the light. Count your blessings each day and rely on the ultimate truth that awaits us one beautiful day.

Like the apostle Paul, we are supposed to sport our weaknesses with our chins up. By the grace and empowerment of the Lord God, we can help others in need because of what we have already walked through. Chin up, Mama. The Lord wants to use you and your testimony for His plans.

When your circumstances surround you in a sea of fog and you are unsure why God would allow something terrible or painful to happen upon you, remain sure of this: "'My grace is sufficient for you.'" We don't have to be ashamed of our pasts, our struggles, or our pain. By the grace of the Lord Jesus, we are covered in full. The Lord wants to use you and your broken pieces for His purposes. Chin up.

Steps of Faith

- Pray this prayer:

  > *Dear Jesus,*
  >
  > *Thank You for Your grace, which comforts and carries me. Thank You for surrounding me with Your love and protection. I pray that Your peace would envelop my daily life and that Your hope would fortify me. Thank You, God, for the solace and assurance that can be found through Your Word. Thank You for Your Holy Presence, which is the ultimate remedy to my anxieties, fears, and weaknesses. Thank You for strategically placing people in my life to uplift and encourage me. In Jesus' almighty name, amen.*

- Meditate on 2 Corinthians 4:16-17: "Therefore we do not lose heart. Though outwardly we are wasting away, yet inwardly we are being renewed day by day. For our light and momentary troubles are achieving for us an eternal glory that far outweighs them all."

14
The Beauty of His Presence

You open your hand and satisfy the desires of every living thing.
The Lord is righteous in all his ways and faithful in all he does.
The Lord is near to all who call on him, to all who call on him in truth.

Psalm 145:16-18

LIKE MOST MOMS, I AM a multitasker. I delight in listening to podcasts while watching my kids play outside. I soak in a good read while taking a bubble bath. I relish listening to writing tutorials while listing antiques. Sometimes, I tackle the dishes while talking on the phone. I type these words one-handed, toting a baby on my hip. Point taken! But when it comes to feeding my five-month-old a bottle, all of my focus is required. Both hands, both eyes, both ears, and both arms are needed. Feeding my baby calls for my full attention.

I wonder if this bottle-feeding scenario plays out in a similar way when we get in our Bibles and pray. I wonder if God holds us and focuses in on us in an endearing sort of way. I cannot help but believe this to be true. When the Lord fills us with the wisdom of His Word and unveils His heart for us through the Bible, He is holding us close, drawing us near. I feel closer to God and recognize His Spirit flowing within my own, through faithful daily prayer. When I focus my full heart and attention on God, He is able to hold and nourish me.

Go to God in prayer. Ask that He would hold you today and feed you the truth of His Word. Ask for His life-giving presence to be illuminated and unfolded throughout your life. Ask for His sustaining grace to fully encompass your mind, motives, and motions. Seek first the kingdom and God's heart for you (Matt. 6:33). Let prayer be the rain that catalyzes growth and good things in your life.

When we come before God with genuine hearts that want to know and grow in Christ's wisdom, love, and peace, we are filled. God is faithful to satisfy our desperate longings for more of His holy presence. All we have to do is ask, open up our hands, and wait for the rain (Matt. 7:7).

Seek after Jesus with a fervent heart that desires to get to know and grow into His likeness. Seek after Jesus with an expectant heart through prayer. Situate your heart, mind, soul, and strength to be solely, wholly, totally devoted to Jesus. Ask the Lord Almighty to mold and sculpt you into the woman He created you to be before time began (Psalm 139:13-14).

Steps of Faith

Multi-task! The next time you feed your baby, prepare a meal, or do the dishes, pray that the Lord will nourish you and your family spiritually.

- Ask for a special bond to exist between you and Jesus.
- Request that God would place His hand on your children's hearts, that the warmth of His touch might mold their minds and desires into his plans and purposes for their lives.
- Pray that your husband would pursue a passionate relationship with Jesus.

15
What's Your Daily Bread?

*All Scripture is God-breathed and is useful for teaching, rebuking, correcting
and training in righteousness, so that the servant of God may be thoroughly
equipped for every good work.*

2 Timothy 3:16-17

A WRITER FRIEND OF MINE recently asked, "How do you do it?" in regard
to my writing. The question caught me off guard. It caused me to pause a
moment, to ponder the inquiry and come to the conclusion that the Bible
is my backbone. It provides me with the strength and daily sustenance I so
desperately need. Yes, it does fuel my writing, but it does so much more than
that. The Bible reorders my heart and rearranges my daily life to be compatible
with God's preconceived will and plans for me.

The Bible is the Word of God. Jesus often referred to himself as "the
truth" (John 14:6), and the Gospel of John refers to Him as the Word Who
both "was with God, and . . . was God" (John 1:1-3). When we read the Bible, we
are ultimately communing with Christ Himself. This, my friends, is fantastic
news. When we come to know and grow closer to Jesus through His Word,
He breathes life into us and provides us with a lantern to hold and carry
throughout our lives. This lantern is the Word, our beautiful hope-filled
Bibles (Psalm 119:105).

When I feel down and discouraged as a mom, opening up my Bible provides a safe, quiet place. Whatever I am reading has the Divine ability to sustain my heart's needs. It is not a simple, quick fix, but the Word never fails to steep my mind in hope and envelop me with the shield of Christ's peace. When I have done the leg work of digging deep into God's Word through prayerful study, the Word can trigger hope into my heart in an instant through a simple, Spirit-filled verse. Memorizing Scripture is a powerful aid in our faith walks. Write God's Word on your heart with permanent ink.

We all share the common thread of a desperate need for Jesus. Let Jesus' words of truth and light pierce your path. In motherhood and in life, seek God's Word to guard and guide you through tough decisions and tumultuous trails. Allow God's Word to give you peace when your world quakes around you. Allow the living, active, breathing, powerful, life-giving, fruit-bearing, holy Word to surround you on all sides of your life.

We all have choices to make throughout the day. How do you spend your time, talent, and treasure? Seek the Lord in and through these things. Get into your Bible first and foremost. Make God's Word a priority and watch how the Lord miraculously restructures your life and daily decisions, according to His will and purposes.

Motherhood presents lots of choices. If you are anything like me, you might have some random sprints of free time speckled throughout your day. Above all else, choose God's Word. Before scrolling, before dishes, before makeup, coffee, or the news, we need God's Word alive in our lives, moving in our hearts.

Jesus promised that He came "'that they may have life, and have it to the full'" (John 10:10). I feel the weight of this verse when I spend too much time on social media. I struggle with this to a certain degree. I have never been a major proponent of social media; but sometimes, I find myself stuck on Facebook or Instagram, getting sucked into scrolling. While scrolling is not a sin, when the posture of my heart is skewed and positioned to pursue social media before reading God's Word, this presents a serious threat. *Jesus, forgive me.*

Going forward, I must safeguard my time and heart by placing God's Word first on my to-do list. When I am getting into the Word, I am much less likely to fall prey to the idol of social media or anything else that threatens my spiritual well-being. First Peter 4:10-11 encourages us to be faithful stewards of God's grace: "Each of you should use whatever gift you have received to serve others, as faithful stewards of God's grace in its various forms . . . so that in all things God may be praised through Jesus Christ. To him be the glory and the power for ever and ever. Amen."

Every aspect of our lives should praise the Lord. Seek God first. Open your Bible and pray throughout the day. Jesus' presence changes everything.

Steps of Faith

- Pray this prayer:

  Dear Lord,

  Give me strength. Give me vision. Give me wisdom to do Your will. I love You and am grateful for Your Word. Make my life a wellspring that overflows with Your truth. Thank You for Your life-giving presence. Please help me to be a good steward of my time, talent, and treasure. In Jesus' loving name, amen.

- For one day, fast from social media. When you become tempted to click the "F" icon or Instagram app, sneak a peek, and spoil the endeavor, seek Jesus' strength through prayer, or open up God's Word. This will be a challenge for me, as I am sure it is for you, too!

16
Live Chosen

"Before I formed you in the womb I knew you, before you were born I set you apart;
I appointed you as a prophet to the nations."

Jeremiah 1:5

THERE HAVE BEEN MANY TIMES in my life I've felt far from chosen. I can remember as early as elementary school being picked in the final rounds for kickball. My mom signed me up for a modeling summer camp in high school, but I was told early on that I would never be tall enough to be an actual runway model. In seventh grade, I was not picked for the A, B, or C team for school volleyball. I participated in what was peer-coined, "Saturday League." My junior year of high school hit me with a devastating blow when I did not make the cheerleading squad. I was turned down by countless publishers in the early stages of my writing journey. As a new mom, I often felt overlooked, isolated, and alone.

In the aftermath of each of my devastations, I have always been met with an echoing truth: God sees me. He has hand-picked me for His kingdom purposes. Whether or not I realized it through the blur of tears, I have never once been set aside but have always been set apart.

The same is true for you. In whatever you are going through and facing today, God has selected you for a specific, special purpose that only you can carry out. In all your moments of waiting, praying, hoping, dreaming, and crying out to Jesus when life doesn't dispense the promised prize in exchange for the coins you so carefully counted and intentionally inserted, God has been there. He has felt the sting of your blow. He knows the heat of your flushed face and has counted your every tear.

So why? Why would God allow such devastation and pain to transpire? For you to depend on Him and realize your desperate need for Jesus. We all have a God-shaped hole inside of us that only Christ can fill. When we strive to fill our holes with things of the world, we run into a square peg and round hole scenario. Things of the world cannot fill a void that exists in the spiritual realm. People, relationships, and successes cannot quench the parched longings of our souls. Tangible things, achievements, and worldly acceptance will never be able to fix our broken hearts. We will continue to come up empty, until we draw from the well of Christ's living water. It is the only thing that can heal, fill, and satisfy the innermost longings of our spirits.

Maybe you are struggling as a new mom. Maybe you are a more seasoned mom, still struggling. I have found that as moms, our struggles often don't go away but many times metamorphose into new monsters. Jesus is the Answer. He is the Truth, the Antidote to the toxic lies we buy into, the Cure for the murmur that exists in our insufficient hearts. He is the Nourishment our children need. In whatever motherhood trials you face—the day in, day out battles; the health crises; the heart crises; the terrible twos (or threes)—whatever it is for you, take it to Jesus. Nail it to the cross. Lean in and depend on Jesus through prayer.

Jesus sees you, Mama. He hears your every need. Pour your heart out to Jesus, for "he cares for you" (1 Peter 5:7). More than anything, Jesus desires a closeness, an eternal bond, a relationship with us. Relationships require communication. One of the number one reasons marriages fall apart is lack of communication. Jesus will never leave or forsake you (Heb. 13:5), but His desire is for you. He desires your time, heart, and attention. Raise your hallelujahs and your hurts to God, Who sees, heals, and rearranges our broken pieces into brilliant, beautiful testimonies. Our testimonies have the God-orchestrated ability to bring hope and shed light into the lives of others.

Despite your past, despite your future, despite your current circumstances and struggles, lean into Jesus. His heart is for you. He goes before you. His grace is sufficient to carry you (2 Cor. 12:9). *Be held.* In letting go and allowing the current of God's love and grace to carry us, we are free to *live loved.* In welcoming the Savior's love and righteous blood to fully envelop our lives, we choose to *live chosen.*

Steps of Faith

- Have you been dependent on your past experiences or current circumstances to define your happiness? Through Christ, we can have joy despite our circumstances. Recite this prayer. Let it sink down deep into your heart and choose to live chosen today.

> *Jesus,*
>
> *Today I choose to worship You. Despite my surroundings, despite my circumstances, despite my struggles, I choose to honor and praise You with my life. Because of the cross of Christ, I look forward to the rainbow of Heaven. Jesus, You are my ultimate Hope, my light in the dark, my freedom song. I trust in You alone. Help me to live chosen today: free from my past, free from my shame, free from my failures and shortcomings. Thank You for Your forgiveness, for setting me free to live and love abundantly. In Jesus' holy name, amen.*

17
Supermom Syndrome

And my God will meet all your needs according to the
riches of his glory in Christ Jesus.

Philippians 4:19

I HAD MY BABY IN her car seat carrier with one hand, and my big, beloved McAlister's iced tea in the other. I had just had lunch with a friend.

"I'll help you carry your drink to the car." she so kindly offered. "I love your white overalls!" she added.

Of course, being the supermom that I am, I refused her offer. Pulling my keys out of my oversized purse, my drink slipped out of my hand, in slow motion, as I tried with catlike reflexes to retrieve it, to no avail. *Splash! Crash!* Not so catlike after all. My drink exploded on the ground, and ice cubes went everywhere. My poor, sweet baby Madison experienced some collateral damage. I wiped iced tea droplets off her pretty, little face and tried to recollect my drink. There was still about a quarter of the iced tea remaining in the cup, so I took a big swig. Iced tea ran all down my white overalls and body, as an uncomfortable soggy feeling mixed with remorse overtook me. The cup was severely cracked. I looked like a person in an old Gatorade commercial, iced-tea style. All of this could have been prevented were I to have accepted my friend's help.

How often do we do this to God? We insist on our own way, only to learn the hard way. A wise person once told me, "It is okay to depend on other people for help." Such a freeing statement. The more we can learn to accept help from and depend on others, the more we are able to experience God's grace. God places people in our lives and presents situations that require us to step up and out of our comfort zones so that we can bless the lives of others. Oftentimes, we are the giver in these situations; but sometimes, the roles are reversed. When we refuse the blessings of others, we are hindering their ability to carry out God's command and denying them a certain level of joy.

It's time we learn how to accept help. It's time we hang our Supermom capes in the closet and accept kindness and compassion from others and receive grace from our Super God. By accepting the Lord's blessings in our lives, we can "abound in every good work" (2 Cor. 9:8). Only through Christ, by accepting His gifts and assignments, can we reach our full potential as moms and believers.

I am nowhere close to being Supermom, but His "'grace is sufficient for [me]'" (2 Cor. 12:9). Only through Christ's power can my weaknesses be used for His glory. Through submitting, obeying, and yielding to the Lord God in all things, I can walk in tune with the plans, purposes, and grace He has for me.

I am learning it's okay to accept help. It's okay to live in the freedom of knowing I cannot do this mom thing on my own. Learn to depend on other people in your life. In whatever way, shape, or form this looks like for you, accept help. The Lord wants to meet your every need; and sometimes, He uses community to fill this gap. Praise God for the everyday angels Jesus places into our lives.

We were not meant to do this mom thing alone. We were made to thrive surrounded by people. If your family does not live in your city, as mine does not, adopt other people and places to meet this need for you. MOPS, Mother's Day Out, women's Bible study, church, close friends—these are all great outlets that provide a safe community of people who want to step in, help, and support you along the way.

Let people into your life. When we surround ourselves with Christian community and friends who build us up, the Lord is able to construct mansions in our hearts that bless our lives and provide a place of grace for others. Fellowship is a beautiful, God-inspired institution that expands the reach of one's heart, connecting its arteries to another and to the heart of Jesus. Fellowship makes the pulse of our lives more in tune with that of Jesus Christ.

Steps of Faith

- Pray this prayer:

  Dear Jesus,

  Please help me to accept help from others so that I can "abound in every good work," as 2 Corinthians 9:8 declares over the lives of those who live generously. Thank You for giving me all that I need. Please help me be a cheerful giver of the gifts and light You have given me. In Jesus' sanctified name, amen.

- Make plans with a friend who is a believer this week.
- Join a MOPS group or women's Bible study.
- Meditate on the following verse and ask God what this verse should like in your life: "And let us consider how we may spur one another on toward love and good deeds, not giving up meeting together, as some are in the habit of doing, but encouraging one another—and all the more as you see the Day approaching" (Heb. 10:24-25).

18
Way-Maker

Moses answered the people, "Do not be afraid. Stand firm and you will see the deliverance the Lord will bring you today. The Egyptians you see today you will never see again. The Lord will fight for you; you need only to be still."

Exodus 14:13-14

AS MOMS, WE ARE TO have faith. Our job is not to do miraculous things but to be faithful in all things. Our job is not to move mountains but to trust the Mountain Mover. When God calls us to something, we are to listen, obey, and have faith that the Lord will make a way. Through the wilderness and desert seasons of life, the Lord is surely leading us, guiding the way, giving us His light, providing warmth through the night and the relief of shade all of our days. Praise Jesus for His presence. Praise God for strategically routing our ways and coursing our paths to align with His plans and bring glory to His name.

Sometimes, I try to take the wheel of my life out of the Captain's hands. I try to steer my ship and avoid icebergs along the way. On average, 90 percent of an iceberg is submerged. It is of little surprise that my ship goes down shortly after I try to maneuver my own way. God is able to see things that we are not. Life challenges may be a means of keeping us safe. What may seem like the long route might be the Lord's way of guarding our hearts, keeping us humble and reliant on Jesus, or preparing us to be used for God's glory.

Pain serves a purpose; discomfort has a plan. God routes our paths according to His plans and purpose. That purpose will ultimately bring glory to the Captain and may unfold in beautiful ways that were never a part of the original map we so carefully crafted. Trust and obey. When God leads you down a Red Sea road that dead ends at the water, listen for His command to wave your staff over the waters and take heart that God is going to produce a miracle in your life. He was capable of parting the Red Sea for Moses and the Israelites. He is capable of making dry bones come alive. He is capable of making beautiful things out of the dust. He is capable of making beautiful things out of our harsh brush strokes and the muddy messes we make of our lives. He is capable of making beautiful things out of us. His resurrection power can redeem our lives.

When you can't see the way, trust that your Captain knows exactly where you are heading. He goes before you, trails behind you, and walks beside you. The Captain relies on a power much greater than sight, for He is the Giver of sight. He knows the way, for He created it. We serve an omnipotent, omnipresent God Who knows the course of our lives like the back of His hand.

When you don't know where to go or your circumstances seem dimly lit, rely on the light in your life to go before you. When fog envelops your life, have faith that the light is still there up ahead, even though you cannot see it. Rely on the warmth Jesus' love and light provides. Move forward and walk "by faith, not by sight" (2 Cor. 5:7).

Motherhood produces many unknowns and places daily unforeseen obstacles and challenges in our lives. We can handle these things in our own strength or trust in the Source of strength itself. God's "power is made perfect in weakness" (2 Cor. 12:9). When we feel weak or situations seem bleak, we can have full confidence in the Captain and trust that the Way-maker will lead us safely through the perils of life to a glorious destination, where we are able to function fully and be used completely as holy vessels of the Living God. He is refining our hearts, causing us to trust and cling to Him. Our struggles strengthen our faith. Through it all, trust and obey, for the Lord is making a way.

Our routes were created before time began; and the Lord simply wants to lead us through, to have our hearts, for us to trust in Him with full confidence. Trust in your Captain, the good Shepherd, Who wants to lead you to gentle streams and green wildflower-filled meadows (Psalm 23). Trust and obey. God is making a way, even when we cannot see.

In the same way that a seed continues to grow beneath the soil before it emerges from the earth, bears leaves, and buds, God continues to move in our hearts and lives, according to His plans and purposes. Although we are not always blooming, blossoming, and unfolding brilliant petals, the Lord is still sanctifying us, doing His secret holy work, beneath the dirt, in our lives.

Steps of Faith

- As a heart offering and pledge that you are going to trust in the Lord fully and follow God's lead in your life, the next time you tip someone, leave a little extra. Say a prayer in the process and tell Jesus that you want to trust and obey Him in all things.

19
Taming the Tongue

Do not let any unwholesome talk come out of your mouths,
but only what is helpful for building others up according to their needs,
that it may benefit those who listen.

Ephesians 4:29

AS A MOM, IT IS easy to casually talk about others in conversation. My prayer is that we would tread lightly, that we would be mindful of the Holy Spirit and considerate of our words, in light of Christ. Let us only speak words that we would say if that person were present. Let us love others by speaking kindness over peoples' lives all the time. This is an admirable trait. Let us strive for holiness in avoiding the temptation of gossip and slander. Although this is prevalent and happens all around us, let us not partake. Gain and establish the reputation as a trusted, faithful friend and family member by refusing to speak ill of or make questionable statements about others.

Let us represent Jesus well through our words. Let us uplift the world and those around us by having conversations that are full of grace, salt, and light (Col. 4:6). Cultivate the habit of saying something kind about someone else—or nothing at all.

I have to be honest with you; this is a challenge for me, as I am sure it is for you, too! Although we might not blatantly gossip about someone, I have found that the black-and-white boundaries of gossip have some shades of gray. Let us avoid the gray altogether. It is better to remain silent than to dishonor the Father through gossip and slander. According to the Bible, the tongue can be like a small spark that sets an entire forest ablaze (James 3:5). On the contrary, "Gracious words are a honeycomb, sweet to the soul and healing to the bones" (Prov. 16:24).

I believe there is a crown in Heaven for every woman who practices the self-discipline of controlling her tongue. Only by the power of the Holy Spirit is this made possible. We will likely stumble at times, but let us repent and strive to live holy lives of love, uplifting others through our words.

Steps of Faith

- Pray the following prayer:

  Lord Jesus,

  Help me to not partake in gossip or slander. Help me to avoid the gray zones when it comes to gossip. Give me words that edify and uplift others instead. Give me the strength and discernment to shine Your light and be an example to my children as someone who does not speak poorly about others. Thank You for the gift of words, God. Please help me be a faithful steward of the voice You have given me. In Jesus' powerful name, amen.

- Say something kind about someone else today. Encourage a family member or friend through your words, a text, or a written note.

- Consider the following verse in terms of gossip and slander:

  Do you not know that in a race all the runners run, but only one gets the prize? Run in such a way as to get the prize. Everyone who competes in the games goes into strict training. They do it to get a crown that will not last, but we do it to get a crown that will last forever. Therefore I do not run like someone running aimlessly;

I do not fight like a boxer beating the air. No, I strike a blow to my body and make it my slave so that after I have preached to others, I myself will not be disqualified for the prize (1 Cor. 9:24-27).

- Practice thinking about what you are going to say before you say it. Pray that the Holy Spirit would put a baby gate upon your lips to keep you safe from stumbling in this regard!

20
Fully-Encompassed Hearts

Create in me a pure heart, O God, and renew a steadfast spirit within me.

Psalm 51:10

"COLOR IT IN, MOMMY! COLOR it in!" Emma Claire begged.

I began to color in the big purple heart that encapsulated the little, same-shade purple heart that was already colored in.

"Where did the little heart go, Mommy?" she asked me moments later, perplexed by the little heart's disappearance.

When we color in our lives the same shade as the Lord's plan, our heart becomes one with God's own. Through obedience, we can become lost in the sea of His favor and love. By giving God our all in every area of our lives, our hearts match the color of God's own. People will notice Jesus when they look at us if our hearts are the same shade as Christ's righteousness and God's love. When our hearts overlap with God's, they seemingly disappear; and all that remains apparent is Jesus' heart.

Speaking of the soon-to-be-anointed David, Samuel said, "'The Lord has sought out a man after his own heart'" (I Sam. 13:14). Much like King David, we, too, can become women after God's own heart when we live lives full of fervent faith, holy reverence, sold-out devotion, God-honoring humility, genuine repentance, and full-force confidence in the Lord's plans. These were traits that David encompassed, and God destined him with a Divine mission because of it.

Fervent faith means that we are not only hearers, but also doers of the Word (James 1:22). We live for the King and take strides of faith daily, even when no tangible reward is foreseen or any recognition is attached.

Holy reverence means that we live God-honoring lives and reside in the fear of the Lord. "The fear of the Lord" is putting God's opinion first, caring what the Lord will think before anyone else; forsaking our own inclinations—and sometimes, even our hearts' desires—in order to please Jesus and abide by the truth of His Word.

Sold-out devotion means that we live lives of worship. We delve into our Bibles each day, seeking wisdom from the Lord. We intentionally set aside precious moments to pray and continue our conversations with Jesus throughout the day. We dwell on things we are thankful for and park our minds on what is true, noble, right, pure, lovely, admirable, excellent, and worthy of praise (Phil. 4:8).

Humility requires us to lay down our pride in exchange for things that are unseen that matter in the light of eternity. Being humble is the opposite of self-seeking, self-promoting, and self-righteousness. It is promoting the Lord above all else and sporting the attributes of Christ in our daily lives. It may cost us popularity, recognition, and our pride. But in turn, meekness leads to elevation in the Lord's eyes and a closeness with Jesus that is priceless. Walking in humility will mean that at times, we need to confess and repent (I John 1:9). Genuine repentance means that we ask the Lord for forgiveness from our sins and then flee from them. If temptation crops up again, we sprint in the opposite direction into the loving, strong arms of Jesus.

Confidence in the Lord's plans means that we are faithful and obedient in the little things. The baby steps along the way guide us through a purification process that eventually leads us to the place the Lord has for us near green pastures and quiet streams. Sometimes, we are led through pitch-black valleys.

But we can always trust in God's guiding light and the warmth of His torch to lead us safely to the places He has planned. He is not going to teleport us there, but He will always walk lovingly by our side. Mountain high or valley low, the Lord will see us through.

Look for His light in your life. "Look to the Lord and his strength; seek his face always" (1 Chron. 16:11). Lean into Jesus. Lace your life with the attributes of a woman after God's own heart, growing in faith, reverence, devotion, humility, repentance, and confidence in Christ, each new day.

Steps of Faith

- Go to God in prayer.

> *Dear Jesus,*
>
> *Thank You for creating me in Your image. Please help me grow into Your likeness, more and more each day, and fill the shoes You created in advance, specifically for me to step into and walk through life wearing with confidence. Thank You, Jesus, for Your heart for me. Please encapsulate my heart within Your own. I want to be found by becoming lost in Your light. I love You, Lord, with all of my heart. Amen.*

21
Let Your Light Shine

"You are the light of the world. A town built on a hill cannot be hidden.
Neither do people light a lamp and put it under a bowl. Instead they put it on
its stand, and it gives light to everyone in the house. In the same way, let your
light shine before others, that they may see your good deeds and glorify your
Father in heaven."

Matthew 5:14-16

AS MOMS, WE ARE CALLED and commanded to be lights in our homes. Some days might feel dark, drab, and lonely; but as moms in Christ, we have been chosen to reflect light from the source of goodness, purity, and joy. We are called to refract God's light in uniquely beautiful ways for our children and the world to see.

God's Word "is a lamp for [our] feet, a light on [our] path[s]" (Psalm 119:105). If we know and believe in this truth, then we should be in our Bibles, seeking Jesus each day. In order to fully shine His light, we must bask in it ourselves. We must collect the precious rays and absorb the radiant glow in order to be living vessels, carrying God's light within our hearts. Christ's light is our everlasting treasure. We are but fragile jars of clay (2 Cor. 4:7).

We must become avid sunbathers in God's goodness, soaking it in through our Bibles and prayer. In order for our lives and hearts to glow, we must come to know and find solace in His loving, glorious, mercy-filled light. Live a sun-soaked life in Christ Jesus.

Christ's light does miraculous, wonderful works:

- His light brings fullness to our lives.
- His light kindles our hearts with His own.
- His light radiates warmth and goodness unto others.
- His light shines truth and brings peace.
- His light sparks a fire of praise in our hearts.
- His light pierces the darkness of our pain with purpose.
- His light causes sin to scatter.
- His light shines testimony and tribute to Christ in our lives.
- His light gracefully falls on us and gives us hope when we feel lost.
- His light exchanges our worries with worship.
- His light unveils beauty that was once hidden away.
- His light stimulates our minds, enveloping our thoughts in truth.
- His light awakens the passion of God's love inside of us, opening the eyes of our hearts, so that we see things a little more like Jesus each day.

We need to collect our rays from the Source. Christ's light is good. It is pure. It has the ability to make us whole. It has the ability to introduce joy back into our lives. We fully reflect His goodness by basking in the that sun. Read the Bible and pray each day. This is a form of spiritual sunbathing that we need to partake in. It may seem like you don't have the time, but make time. Stop scrolling. Put it at the top of your to-do list. Pencil it in. Do whatever it takes to get into the Word.

My high school cross-country coach often reiterated a quote in regard to being diligent to practice outside of school. "Motivated people find ways," he would say. Motivated mamas find ways! Read your Bible during soccer practice, naptime, before your children wake up, or after they go to sleep. Pray while cooking, doing dishes, feeding the baby, folding laundry, or driving kids to school. Let your light shine for this dark, despondent, in-need-of-Jesus world to see. May your children, and everyone else you encounter in this lifetime, witness the light and warmth of Christ in you.

Steps of Faith

- Pray this prayer:

    Dear Jesus,

    Thank You for Your light in my life. Thank You for the candle of Your Word to illuminate the way, the flame of the Gospel flickering in my life, and the torch of Your Holy Spirit to guide me. "Your word is a lamp for my feet, a light on my path" (Psalm 119:105). For this reason, I forever praise You. In Jesus' holy name, amen.

- Make a plan of action. When will you read your Bible? When will you pray? Some of us have some spare change of free time, while many of us do not. We are still called and commanded to strive after the heart of Christ in our daily lives. Maybe you need to invest in another Bible to keep with you in your car for reading (while parked) when waiting for your kids to get out of school, or during after school activities. Make time, not excuses. We all find ways to do things that we really and truly love that our hearts crave. Make Jesus a priority, and your love and desire for Him will grow and glow throughout your life.

22

Press In

*But you are a chosen people, a royal priesthood, a holy nation, God's special
possession, that you may declare the praises of him who called you out of
darkness into his wonderful light.*

1 Peter 2:9

JESUS IS THE ANSWER. HE is the Answer to our pain, struggle, purpose,
and heartache. He has the ability to connect the dots in our lives that enable
us to experience "Aha!" moments through Scripture. He has the ability to
heal our brokenness and seal our gaping wounds. Jesus has the ability to
restore. In whatever you walk through today, press into Jesus; for "He cares
for you" (1 Peter 5:7).

We all walk through death, experience tragedies, wade through sorrows,
and struggle through the drought of disappointment in our lives. We can all
relate to these tumultuous trials in some way, shape, or form. A blaring siren
sounds in the back of our minds, recalling our former difficult seasons that
haunt and threaten to encapsulate us in a wave of remembering, an undertow
of regret. But many times, we can look back and see the wonder-working
power of the cross in our lives, orchestrated through these difficult chapters.
Jesus was somehow glorified; our relationship with Him was renewed;
friendships were restored—all through these dark valleys.

In the early days of my writing career, I made little-to-no money. Some years, I spent more money to fund my writing endeavors than what I actually made. Yet I could not snuff out the spark of passion God placed inside of me. I did try for a period of time, as logic and reason deemed it was a waste of time. But one day, I could sense my Savior say, "Keep on writing for Me like it's your job." There was no promise attached to this mandate, but I have been called and am going to walk in obedience mountain high or valley low in my writing career.

Oftentimes in Scripture, obedience precedes miracles. I am leaning in on this truth, pressing through the darkness, writing in faith with an expectant heart, knowing the Lord is able to do big things with my little pen. I write not for fame or monetary gain but to glorify God and make Jesus' name known, to draw my heart closer to His own. My prayer is that my words inspire other women to scoot a little bit closer to Jesus as well.

When your situation seems hopeless, useless, and less than, know that you serve a God Who is greater than. He is greater than your weakness. He is greater than your ideal self. He is greater than your pain and struggle. When you become helpless or circumstances surround you in a sea of darkness, look for the light. God is still good, even when our situations stink. And sometimes, they do! As moms, we struggle just like anybody else. We struggle with purpose, identity, self-image, and wanting to be recognized and appreciated for all that we do.

God is still good. His purposes are pure. God wants to walk us through a refining process through motherhood that draws us closer to His heart. When we wrap our arms around Jesus, we become in tune and in touch with the heartbeat of God. We can feel His heart beating throughout our lives when we press into Jesus through God's Word, avid prayer, and giving thanks, dwelling on all that is pure, lovely, admirable, true, noble, and right (Phil. 4:8). Press into Jesus and feel the rhythm of God's heart beating throughout your life.

You are a chosen, royal priesthood; a daughter of the King (1 Peter 2:9). Put on your crown, set your hands to the task and press into all that the Lord God has for you.

Steps of Faith

- Pray the following:

  Jesus,

  Open the eyes of my heart so that I can gain purpose, glean wisdom, and accumulate insight through the wonder working power of Your presence in my daily life. Through my difficult circumstances, empower me by Your truth. Inspire me with Your love. Infuse me with Your hope. Encourage me by Your grace. Engulf me in Your goodness. Rapture my heart with Your peace. In Jesus' resurrected name, amen.

- What area of your life do you need to surrender over to Jesus?
- In what way has God called you for His kingdom purposes? How can you make Jesus' name known?

23
Uplifted by Christ's Yoke

"Take my yoke upon you and learn from me,
for I am gentle and humble in heart, and you will find rest for your souls.
For my yoke is easy and my burden is light."

Matthew 11:29-30

WITH A BABY CRYING FOR her bottle, two toddlers demanding lunch, a stinky diaper to change, and groceries to carry in, my state of adrenaline kicked in. But I felt a wave of "this mom gig is too much" crash over me, threatening to take me down. In panicked, crazy moments of motherhood, my patience seems to dwindle; and sometimes, if I am being completely honest, I would like to run and hide.

The truth is, some days, I feel like I am just barely squeaking by. I run around threadbare, living off fumes, fighting for my sanity, while deep down desperately wanting to do a good job. But when I go to God in prayer, He takes my burden and replaces my overwhelmed feelings with the yoke of His sustaining peace. We can be accompanied by Christ's yoke by staying connected to the source of God's truth through our Bibles, prayer, and faith checkpoints throughout the day.

The other day, I was jogging around a church that is near our neighborhood. This church has a track built around its perimeter so that walkers, joggers, and bikers have a safe place to land. Around the track are Bible verses on yard signs. One of the verses is Romans 14:12: "So then, each of us will give an account of ourselves to God." This verse is a great reminder that whatever we do, whether in public or private, we will have to give an account of ourselves to God, down to every little detail of our lives.

When I jog around this church, I make a point to listen to Christian music. Listening to Christian music lightens and refreshes my soul. It is one way that I take upon Christ's yoke. Right now, Brandon Lake is my jam! The lyrics of his song "Gratitude" are life-giving, soul-refreshing, and powerful. When motherhood and life become all too much to carry, the lyrics of this song come to mind and empower me. The lyrics allude to the fact that we are not enough in and of ourselves, but all that we have is a "Hallelujah." Our praise is precious in God's sight and more than enough.

When our arms are too full and our plates are overflowing, let us lean into God's grace and promises. Our desire should be to be faithful in all things as mothers, wives, and daughters of Christ. But when we are doing our best and our best doesn't feel good enough, Christ's grace covers our inadequacies. The Lord is pleased by our efforts to live for Him and represent Jesus well in all things.

As moms, sometimes we will feel overwhelmed and shorthanded. Christ's grace can fill the gaps. Never give up because the Jesus you are yoked to is willing to do anything and everything it takes to see you through all that He has called you to.

Steps of Faith

- Write a prayer that God would equip you by His power and might to be the best mom and godly wife that you can be, all for His glory. Here is an example:

  Dear Jesus,
  Embolden me with Your strength, vision, and resurrection power to fight against my flesh tendencies of laziness,

self-centeredness, and lack of zeal. Motivate me through Your Word to do Your will. God, I want to be the best mom I can be, all for Your glory. Equip me for Your kingdom purposes. Empower me to live and love a little more like You each day. In Jesus' flawless name I pray, amen.

- Listen to the song "Gratitude" by Brandon Lake today.

24
The Lord Bless You and Keep You

The Lord said to Moses, "Tell Aaron and his sons, 'This is how you are to bless the Israelites. Say to them: ""The Lord bless you and keep you; the Lord make his face shine on you and be gracious to you; the Lord turn his face toward you and give you peace."' So they will put my name on the Israelites, and I will bless them."

Numbers 6:22-27

THE BOOK OF NUMBERS CONSISTS of a wide variety of intricate ordinances that were intended to help the Israelites love God and live holy lives. But when we come to the end of chapter six, verses twenty-two through twenty-seven, there is a delightful surprise of the Lord's instructions to Aaron for how to pray over the children of Israel. We can adopt the model of these verses to pray for our own children as well.

To "make His face shine upon you" depicts an illustration of someone experiencing peace, joy, and all-consuming love in the Lord's presence. For the Lord to "lift up His countenance upon" someone implies that the person has found favor in the Lord's sight. We can experience the sensation of God's face shining upon us through basking in His presence by reading our Bibles and seeking Jesus in prayer. Through steadfast obedience and listening to the Holy Spirit's heart promptings throughout the day (*befriend that lonely mother, give that barista a tip, reach out to that acquaintance, speak a verse over your children, pray with your kids on the way to school),* we can become women who are in tune and in touch with the heart of God. By relying on His presence in our lives, we become women after God's own heart, ready and equipped to conquer the world in Jesus' name. When we are obedient to God, He is pleased and "lifts up His countenance upon" us.

When my children do extraordinary things, I am naturally proud of them. But even in ordinary, day-to-day moments, I am a proud mama. My children don't have to "impress" me for my countenance to shine upon them, it just naturally does. However, when my children disappoint me through sin and disobedience, it makes my heart sad.

I cannot help but believe that God operates in a similar way. We do not have to earn His approval to be called His children. We were adopted into His family the moment we accepted Jesus into our hearts. The Lord is pleased with us naturally, and there's nothing we have to do to earn His approval. There may be moments in our lives that we can feel His countenance shine upon us more than others, but God's love never lets go. He holds us in the palm of His hand. As His children, God loves us thoroughly and completely.

When we mess up and sin, God is disappointed; and we feel that through the consequences of our actions. But the Lord is full of mercy and grace and is quick to forgive. When we come to Jesus with sincere, repentant hearts, we are able to set our relationship with the Lord right. We are forgiven in full when we ask.

God equips us to make better future choices through the Divine direction of His Word. It can be alive and active in our hearts, "sharper than any double-edged sword" (Heb. 4:12) when wielded with the power and authority of the Holy Spirit governing our hearts and hands.

Let the Lord's countenance shine upon you through steadfast obedience and daily diligence to get in the Word and seek Christ through prayer. Read your Bible with a "Lord shine down on me" mindset and an expectant heart.

Steps of Faith

- Pray this prayer over your children, based on Numbers 6:24-26:

  Lord,

  Bless my little ones and keep them. May Your face shine upon them and pour out Your graciousness over their lives. Lord, lift up Your countenance upon my children and encompass them with Your all-consuming peace. Amen.

25
love and light

Give thanks to the Lord, for he is good. His love endures forever. *Give thanks to the God of gods.* His love endures forever. *Give thanks to the Lord of lords:* His love endures forever. *To him who alone does great wonders,* His love endures forever.

Psalm 136:1-4

RESILIENCE—SUCH A PROFOUND WORD. GOD is constantly echoing this word throughout the chorus of my life, emboldening my faith along the way. During this season of mothering littles, I hear this word whispered often and unexpectedly: when the marker streaks are found on the walls, through my toddlers' whining and the baby's constant crying, I can still hear my Savior's voice telling me it's all going to be okay. And then there are some moments that catch me off guard, leaving me breathless, in awe of the awesome, wonderful God we call Abba Father: my two-year-old quietly singing "Jesus loves me this I know"; my daughter looking up from playing, locking eyes with mine, and telling me fiercely, "I love you, Mommy." Yes, some moments are there to remind me that motherhood matters. God has planted and placed all that we need to live lives of abundance, growing our faith and fortifying our resilience when we have hearts of gratitude.

How can we cultivate the seeds of gratitude in our hearts? Through tangibly, literally, and physically praising the Lord, coming before Jesus in prayer, and mentioning our thanks in specific ways, we exercise the muscle of thankfulness. This muscle can carry us through tough times and dark days when well-conditioned and trained.

The conditioning is not always easy, as some moments seem to be covered by a cloud of chaos, confusion, and negative thoughts. But our Redeemer lives. He has called us out of darkness to dance in His marvelous light.

According to Christ, we are chosen, called, made to praise, reflections of his royalty, made holy through his blood (1 Peter 2:9). Because of Jesus, we have a purpose for joy and a reason for gratitude. I echo the words of Paul, "For me, to live is Christ" (Phil. 1:21). Jesus is my sole Purpose in life. When I remember this truth—that Jesus is my Everything—the strings of my heart readjust, and the priorities of my life untangle as Christ's kingdom purposes carry me.

Being thankful takes strength. It takes strength of heart. It takes strength of mind. It takes strength of will and continuous heart recalibration. To choose to dwell on our thanksgivings before our grudges takes focus and consistent persistence in looking for the light. When we position the arrows of our lives away from ourselves and upward toward Heaven, Jesus redirects our aim and enables us to hit the bullseye of being the most glorifying, faith-filled daughters of the King that we can be.

Having a heart of thanksgiving is only possible through the funnel of the Holy Spirit. Jesus is able to strain out our negativity by means of His truth, God's Word, and through His consummate power that is able to meet us in our weakness and bridge the gap of our ill-equipped hearts with His divine strength (2 Cor. 12:9).

Rely on Jesus' strength. Make cognizant heart shifts that position you toward the light in your life, away from darkness, negativity, selfishness, and small-minded thoughts. While in prison, Paul penned this message to the church of Colossae: "Set your minds on things above, not on earthly things. For you died, and your life is now hidden with Christ in God. When

Christ, who is your life, appears, then you also will appear with him in glory"
(Col. 3:2-4). Shift your mind to Heaven. Through Christ's strength we can be
covered and carried in love and light.

Steps of Faith

- Praise Jesus for five to ten things you are thankful for today.
  Maybe these are blessings you often take for granted and want to
  make a conscious effort to thank Jesus for. Make a list of these
  things. Write them down and refer to them often.
- Read through Psalm 136:23-26. Prayerfully reflect on the fact that
  God is good, unchanging, faithful, our Redeemer, and eternally
  thank-worthy.

26
Your Will Be Done

"Father, if you are willing, take this cup from me; yet not my will,
but yours be done."

Luke 22:42

THE LORD HAS BEEN CHALLENGING me to adopt a "Not my will, but your will be done, Father" attitude lately. Jesus spoke these world-renowned words in the Garden of Gethsemane hours before His crucifixion. His words set the bar for us as believers. This mindset is not always the easy way. We know from Scripture that living a righteous life dedicated to Christ requires sacrifice—sacrifice to self, sacrifice of creature comforts, sacrifice to distractions, sacrifice of anything and everything that takes away from us living sold-out lives for Jesus.

Every day, we are faced with choices. When we prayerfully seek Jesus through these choices, God enables us to choose His will. Before reaching for your phone, focus on your kids. Before you look at social media, read God's Word. Before you clean your house or do the laundry, examine the conditions of your heart. (I preach these words to myself, more than anyone else.)

The truth is, sometimes, I use my phone as a means of escape. I resort to folding laundry before scrutinizing the orderliness of my heart. I have committed scandals of looking at social media or checking emails before checking in with God's Word. I am a flawed human being as much as anybody else. But we have been called to live set-apart lives.

As followers of and believers in Jesus, we are to lead holy lives. I am not saying that all things phone-oriented are against God's will or that folding laundry is a bad thing. What I am saying is that there is a time and a place for every different component of our lives (Eccles. 3:1). How we spend our time and the order in which we prioritize often indicates what we treasure. This is something we should grapple with as believers looking to sanctify and refine our lives according to Jesus' standards so that we can be used as holy vessels for His kingdom purposes.

In the little things and the large, I want to be used by Jesus. I want every area of my life to please my Lord and Savior. I want all chambers of my heart to be open to His will. I want all pieces of my mind to reflect His glory.

Jesus wants us to adopt His model of a well-balanced life that's focused on the Lord. Luke 2:52 illustrates the different facets of how Jesus grew: "in wisdom and stature, and in favor with God and man." We need to reorient our lives to look a little more like Jesus each day.

I've heard it said that healthy things grow. We need to grow in our knowledge of Scripture and tuck the truth and treasure of God's Word into our hearts. We need to take care of our bodies as temples of the Holy Spirit. We need to live in the fear of the Lord, seeking to do the Lord's will and walk close to Christ daily. We must establish friendships that build us up and fortify our faith. Wisdom, stature, in favor with God and man—seek to abide by the Spirit of the Living God, and grow in truth, each new day.

Steps of Faith

- Pray the following:

  Father, Your will be done in my heart and life. I want to abide in Your holy presence. Lead me by Your Spirit. Teach me to be a good listener. Help me to obey, no matter what the circumstance. I want to do Your will in all things. Show me ways to grow in wisdom, stature, in favor with God, and man. In Jesus' righteous name, amen.

27

New Morning Mercies

Because of the Lord's great love we are not consumed, for his compassions
never fail. They are new every morning; great is your faithfulness.

Lamentations 3:22-23

PURSUING CROSSFIT RIGHT AFTER COLLEGE, I quickly became in the best shape of my life. I remember doing actual pushups, many of them. My muscles would become fatigued during my workouts to a point that my arms would actually give out; and there I would lie, face down on the gym floor, until I had resurrected enough strength to try again. Sometimes, I feel this same repetitive strengthening as I go about loving and caring for my children each day. Not all moments are pleasant; and some require I call upon the patience of the Lord, remembering His patience for me.

When life seems too much to bear and our mama muscles give in, we are still held in Jesus' loving arms. We can lie on the gym floor and rest, knowing the plans He has for us are good, even when the conditioning is hard work.

When we experience "mom fails" (we all experience these from time to time), Jesus gives us grace and new strength to try again. The Holy Spirit infuses us with Divine courage to start anew when we mess up and muddle the brilliant colors of our lives to create a shade of muddy brown because of our sin and selfish tendencies. "'[Christ's] power is made perfect in [our] weakness'" (2 Cor. 12:9). Jesus' unfailing strength can pull us through and enable us to cross the finish line of the goals, plans, and purposes He has for us, in stride.

When mess-ups, hardship, and sorrows surround us, Christ anchors our hearts near the lighthouse of hope found in God's truth. When we read God's loving Word, we realize that the plans and purposes the Lord has for us are good. Jesus is able to swap our drab, despondent perspectives with the illuminating light of His hope, reminding us of His love, character, and heavenly goodness when we call upon Christ through prayer. The Holy Spirit intercedes on our behalf when we don't know what to pray. It's okay to simply say, "Jesus, help me." God alone is able to envelop us in His holy peace, comfort our weary hearts, and carry our heavy burdens.

Being a mom requires us to lay down our lives (John 15:13) and "love [our] neighbor as [ourselves]" (Mark 12:31). Our neighbors are our children, the ones we do life with and next to every day. I am nowhere near perfect in this way; but if we can take baby steps toward loving our little ones in a similar way that Christ loved us—to the point of death on a cross—then we are doing a God-honoring job.

This is our role as mothers in Christ—to love our little ones with all of our might. We feed, nourish our souls, and take care of our bodies every day. We must strive to love our children to the best of our God-given abilities and pray that the Holy Spirit will meet us halfway.

On the days that seem like more weight than what our feeble arms and hearts can bear, may we call upon Christ's strength. May we go to God in prayer and rest a moment on the gym floor until Christ's resurrection power infuses us with the Divine ability to stand, to start again, to pursue Christ's holiness, and chase after glorifying God. His mercies can cover and carry us when we realize our desperate need and come before Jesus with contrite, humble hearts.

Steps of Faith

- Pray this prayer:

  Dear Jesus,

  You give me all the strength that I need to pursue a life of godliness, a lifestyle of love. Infuse me with more of You. Forgive me when I fail and give me new strength to try again. Thank You for Your grace that envelops me. In Jesus' loving name, amen.

- Do some pushups or something that is challenging today and reflect on the fact that motherhood is hard work but that Christ's strength gives us all that we need.

- Read the following as a benediction and call to action over your life:

  Now may the God of peace, who through the blood of the eternal covenant brought back from the dead our Lord Jesus, that great Shepherd of the sheep, equip you with everything good for doing his will, and may he work in us what is pleasing to him, through Jesus Christ, to whom be glory for ever and ever. Amen (Heb. 13:20-21).

28
Be Strong in the Lord

"Be strong and courageous. Do not be afraid or terrified because of them,
for the Lord your God goes with you; he will never leave you nor forsake you."

Deuteronomy 31:6

MY SON AND DAUGHTER WERE soaring through the air on the disk swing in our backyard, having the time of their lives. Emma started scooting around on the swing, trying to get a better grasp on the ropes. As a result, Josiah got knocked off the swing. This is probably starting to sound like an innocent accident, which it was. But that did not change the fact that Josiah fractured his leg when he fell!

When Eve ate the fruit in the Garden of Eden, she failed to perceive the long-term effects. Sin is sin. Adam and Eve's sin broke our relationship with God. While it would be easy to point fingers and blame Eve, we fall prey to sin in similar ways.

As moms, it is easy to wish for a shinier, more glamorous lifestyle. We see the fruit, and it looks good. But when we buy into the lie and take a bite, we find that the consequences outweigh the fruitions of our sinful desires. Having longings and life wishes is not a sin, but discontentment poses a real threat in our lives. It can cause us to veer away from God's perfect plan and take matters into our own hands.

The plans God has for us are good (Jer. 29:11). They might not be glittery, always happy, or stress-free. This is not a guarantee. But the plans God has for us are intended to lead us to green pastures and quiet streams (Psalm 23). We might have to walk through some dark valleys to get there but lean in. Cling tightly to your faith. Look for the light in your life—the blessings and the light of Christ. We have an everlasting hope because of Jesus. Trust that God is going to lead you through the difficult moments and trying times in motherhood to a place of peaceful waters. Allow motherhood to strengthen you. Refuse to fall prey to the traps and temptations Satan strategically places along the way. Stick to what is true, noble, right, pure, and lovely in Jesus' sight (Phil. 4:8).

After three weeks in a cast, my son's leg healed. Jesus came to mend and restore our forever relationship with the Lord God. Jesus was the Sacrifice for what should have been our cross to bear. Through Jesus, we are offered grace and forgiveness in full. The free gift of salvation is ours to behold. We should cherish this precious gift because of the monumental sacrifice that was made—all because of love, all because of Jesus.

We must live lives of obedience and gratitude because of God's great love for us in sending His treasured Son. We live lives of sold-out faith through fully trusting in and relying on Jesus' consummate strength.

Steps of Faith

- Pray this prayer:

  Dear Jesus,

  Help me to be a woman of Your Word. Teach me to dwell on the truths You have spoken over my life. "You knit me together in my mother's womb" (Psalm 139:13). I am "a chosen . . . royal priesthood" (1 Peter 2:9), created in advance for good works. Help me to be content in this season and remind me of Your light in my life when I feel discouraged. Give me Your courage. Give me Your strength. In Jesus' everlasting name, amen.

- The next time you push your kids on the swing or watch them play, thank God for the day and mention any other thanksgivings that come to mind. Cultivate a mindset of gratitude by counting your blessings and praising God each day.

29
Raising Healthy Children Who Love Jesus

Fix these words of mine in your hearts and minds; tie them as symbols on your hands and bind them on your foreheads. Teach them to your children, talking about them when you sit at home and when you walk along the road, when you lie down and when you get up. Write them on the doorframes of your houses and on your gates.

Deuteronomy 11:18-20

"YOU'RE IN THE THICK OF it!" I was recently told.

We were having a family gathering; and not only were my little children present but also my brother's three kids of similar ages (six years old and under). Parents were trying to throw food on plates for little mouths, and children were running around like wild banshees. Things were *busy.*

Yes, I am! I thought to myself.

Only later did I realize the essence of what being "in the thick of it" meant for me as a mom from a spiritual point of view.

As mamas of littles, we play a salient role. Our children are walking through crucial developmental years. Our job as Christian mamas is to raise healthy children who love Jesus. Less than a week had passed since that family gathering when I was confronted head-on with some biblical truths found in Deuteronomy about parenting. Some factors that enable children to properly grow and become fully functioning adults include:

1. Unconditional Love
2. Discipline
3. Consistency
4. Parents' example
5. Bonding with a healthy male and female authority figure

These factors are based on psychiatric research but are also supported with biblical evidence. Let's look at each component individually.

1. Unconditional Love: God demonstrates his unconditional love to us daily, through mercy and forgiveness, through Jesus. We are to forgive our children in full when they sin. We are to be merciful parents who relay God's unconditional love into our children's lives.

2. Discipline: Discipline equals discipleship. The way that we discipline our children can speak volumes of God's love, justice, grace, and forgiveness. When we discipline through the lens of Christ Jesus, not sparing the rod but being quick to love our children afterward, the gospel message of Jesus' forgiveness and God's grace is relayed into our children's hearts.

3. Consistency: We must be consistent disciplinarians. This helps our children feel safe, confident, and secure. Do not turn a blind eye at an offense one day and then lash out on your child the next. We have to be consistent in our approach so that our children's little hearts are moved toward Jesus through the process of discipline. We must be consistent in discipling our children through reading God's Word, talking about Jesus, singing praise and worship songs, and praying. Many times throughout the book of Numbers and Deuteronomy, the Israelites were commanded to pass on God's truth and the legacy of his greatness to their children and grandchildren (Deut. 4:9). We must infuse our children's minds and hearts with God's love in this same powerful way.

4. Parents' Example: The Israelites were commanded to obey. This set an example for their children of what living out God's truth and walking in obedience should look like. We must obey God's Word and set an example of godliness for our children.

5. Bonding: My kids love trains. I remember once telling my husband that I felt like I was not good at playing trains. He told me to get down on the floor and do it anyway. Get down on the floor, play with, and have conversations with your children each day. Your relationship with your child will thrive when you go the extra mile in this way.

Properly nurturing children in their developmental years is crucial. As a mother, this is one of our greatest jobs—to nurture and see to the growth of our children. This is a major responsibility that we should reflect on frequently. We must desire and strive to do our best in raising healthy, godly children. We should pray daily that the Holy Spirit will ultimately nurture their hearts and guide their footsteps to the cross.

Steps of Faith

- Pray the following:

  > *Lord Jesus,*
  > *I pray that my children will grow up to be healthy, godly adults who love You with all their hearts. Guide me as a parent. Give me wisdom. In Jesus' holy name, amen.*

- Reflect on the five factors of raising children to become healthy adults: unconditional love, discipline, consistency, parents' example, and bonding with a healthy male and female authority figure. Make a game plan for which area you would like to work on and improve. Make your game plan specific. Be intentional to follow through.

30
Motivated Mama

He humbled you, causing you to hunger and then feeding you with manna,
which neither you nor your ancestors had known, to teach you that man does not
live on bread alone but on every word that comes from the mouth of the Lord.

Deuteronomy 8:3

"MOMMY, WILL YOU READ TO me these Jesus books?" my sweet girl asked me, coming down the stairs from her rest time.

I was starstruck and overjoyed at the same time. You see, for a good, long while, it had felt like I was driving the horse of reading the Bible with my kids each day. At times, it felt like that horse did not want to budge. Or I would lead it to water but couldn't make it drink. So when my daughter dawdled down the stairs to ask me if we could read "Jesus books" (which were, in fact, children's Bibles), I was elated.

We have to consistently impress God's Word into our children's hearts. We do this through exposure. We do this through consistency. We do this through prayer and relying on the Holy Spirit to move in our children's spirits. It might feel like your kids don't care or aren't paying attention when you read God's Word, but I promise they hear every word that rolls off your lips. They absorb more than you realize.

As moms, if we don't read God's Word to our kids, chances are that no one will. This is the sad, blunt truth. We must be persistent. We must be diligent.

We must be faithful in reading the Bible with our children. Galatians 6:9 promises us, "Let us not become weary in doing good, for at the proper time we will reap a harvest if we do not give up."

Our children's hearts are hungry for the Word of God. We have the ability and God-given responsibility to bless our children in this way. Is there grace when we fail to read God's Word to our children? Some days, "busy" is not just an excuse but a reality. There is grace. But on most days, motivated mamas find ways!

Whether we realize it or not, the Holy Spirit is moving in our children's lives. We must be diligent and faithful with the littles seeds of our children's hearts that the Lord has entrusted to us. God is ultimately in control of our children's faith (praise the Lord!) But we have a salient role to play.

Read the Bible and pray with your children. Give them the opportunity to pray. For Jesus said, "'Let the little children come to me, and do not hinder them, for the kingdom of heaven belongs to such as these'" (Matt. 19:14). Give your children opportunities to come to Jesus each day.

Steps of Faith

- Pray this prayer:

  Dear Jesus,

  Please help me to be faithful to prepare my children's hearts to receive You by reading Your Word with them daily. Give me diligence and discipline in this endeavor. Holy Spirit, move in my children's hearts. Instill in them a desire to know You and to love You. Plant a purpose inside of them that whispers Your name. In Jesus' precious, powerful, and perfect name I pray, amen.

- Tonight at bedtime, pray with your children. Then ask them to pray. Create a habit of daily prayer.

- Purchase a children's Bible if you do not already own one. Simply pick one that resonates with your heart.
- If you already own a children's Bible but desire to read it with your children more often, relocate it. Pull it out. Place it within sight. Keep it somewhere where you will be reminded to read it each day.

31
Strong Mom

Righteousness and justice are the foundation of your throne;
love and faithfulness go before you. Blessed are those who have learned to
acclaim you, who walk in the light of your presence, Lord.

Psalm 89:14-15

SO OFTEN IN MOTHERHOOD AND life, I try to do things on my own. I try to mom alone. I run in my own strength. I forget to acknowledge God throughout the day. All too often, I forget to fully rely on my Jesus who is quick to provide His love and faithfulness in full. When I am confronted with a dead end and cry out to Jesus, God whispers His name upon my heart. He meets me at my point of weakness and commands me to move out of the way and just let the Way-maker through.

When we submit our lives and hearts to the only One Who can make a way, we are accepted into Jesus' loving embrace. He is with us always but is better able to carry us through when we rise up and say yes to all that He has called us to. We must lean in and listen for His voice with acute care and prayerful expectancy.

God parts the Red Seas in our lives but sometimes calls us out into the wilderness to wander a while to regain our strength and reliance on the Lord. This wilderness-wandering refocuses our sights to be fixed and focused on Christ, to rely on His cloud cover by day and the warmth of His fire by night.

Jesus' presence changes everything and causes even our most desperate, desolate seasons to transform into desert rose blessings that bloom over time. Sometimes, what seems like a wilderness season is God's way. Its purpose might be for us to realize our desperate need, to reset our hearts, and to rely on Jesus with all of our heart, mind, soul, and strength.

In the words of Ruth Schwenk, "Our hearts will always be restless and wandering until we learn that only hungering and thirsting for God will truly satisfy."[3] That is quite the oxymoron! In order to be filled, we must pour ourselves out. In order to experience abundance, we must taste our desperate need for Christ.

Jesus offers us His very own righteousness through His blood (Rom. 3:24); but sometimes, we must march through the consequences of our sin. When we form a blockade through our self-reliance and unwillingness to yield to God's way, the Way-maker will still get us to the destination He has planned; but it may require a longer, more scenic route. This "scenic route" is often way less scenic and more desert-like in nature. Sometimes, the "scenic route" teaches us a lesson in the long run—to choose God's way first; to say, "Yes Lord, have your way"; and to be quick to obey. Most of all, the scenic route gives us time to grapple with the fact that we need Jesus. We need Jesus desperately. We need Jesus fully. We need Jesus, forever and always. We need Jesus, plain and simple.

Sometimes, the Lord asks things of us that seem like "big asks." It takes great faith to be bold when these mountains are placed before us. But when we remember Who made those mountains, Who has the ability to move them and even toss them into the sea, we are able to see a bit more clearly. When we rely on God's character of righteousness, justice, love, and faithfulness (Psalm 89:14), we can see past our own vantage points through the telescopic lens of Christ Jesus.

We all must walk through hard things in motherhood and life. These tough moments mold us to be more like Christ and make us more resilient

---

3   Ruth Schwenk, *The Better Mom Devotional* (Grand Rapids: Zondervan, 2018), 61.

in our faith (James 1:3). Through the strengthening of our faith and character, we become strong moms.

A "strong mom" is different from what you would expect. A strong mom is not one who does things all by herself and muscles her way through motherhood and life. A strong mom lays down her life for her children and family each day. She realizes that what she does is special and has value in Jesus' sight. A strong mom has a meek and humble spirit, who knows that her purpose and identity is rooted in Christ alone. A strong mom is fully reliant on the presence of Jesus. Her strength is found in Christ alone. A strong mom is quick to get out of the way and let the Way-maker have His way in her heart and life.

Steps of Faith

- In what way can you be a "strong mom" today?
- Write out a prayer that boldly approaches the throne of God's grace and inquire what His plans and purposes for you are. Ask Him to make you a strong mom, humbly equipped and wholeheartedly reliant on Jesus.

32
live Bold

"You are a king, then!" said Pilate. Jesus answered, "You say that I am a king.
In fact, the reason I was born and came into the world is to testify to the truth.
Everyone on the side of truth listens to me."

John 18:37

HAVE YOU EVER HAD TO choose between the truth of God's Word and
the tidal wave force of the crowd? Like the decision Pilate faced in whether
to release or condemn Jesus, we, too, have decisions to make that require us
to stand up, stick out, walk the extra mile, and swim against the school of
popularity in our lives.

Pilate was the Roman governor of Judaea between the approximate years
of 26-37 CE. CE stands for "common era." I grew up with the knowledge of
BC, "before Christ," and AD, *"anno Domini,"* which means "in the year of the
Lord," as the standard time period referrals. Oh, how the history books have
changed! They have taken Christ out of the equation. In doing so, the world
has tried to turn a blind eye and detract merit from the truth of all that Christ
was, is, and continues to be as King of the world and Savior of our hearts.

Similar to changing the abbreviations of BC to BCE and AD to CE, Pilate
tried to sweep what he was doing in allowing Christ to be condemned under
the rug. He tried to pass the baton before the blood fell on his hands. We, too,
can commit sin and wrong choices when we know and are convicted of the

right thing to do and simply choose not to do it. Obedience is a choice, and it is possible to passively disobey.

Pilate was convinced that Jesus was the Messiah. He knew in his heart what the decision should be (John 18:38). Even so, he allowed his beliefs to be bulldozed by popular opinion (John 19:12). When we feel the Holy Spirit's promptings in our lives, we must choose to listen to the truth and obey. If we believe in our hearts that Jesus is Lord, we must accept His daily assignments as King of our lives. Jesus said, "'I am the way and the truth and the life. No one comes to the Father except through me'" (John 14:6). There's no other way to be reunited with our Heavenly Father except through Jesus. Furthermore, Jesus is the Truth, the Living Word (John 1:1-3). When we read the Bible, we are ultimately communing with Christ Himself. This, my friends, is fantastic news.

Jesus said, "'Everyone on the side of truth listens to me'" (John 18:37). With Jesus in our hearts, we have the ability to prayerfully and biblically discern the Lord's will in our lives. Praise God for the gift of His Word. Praise God for the gift of His only Son.

When I sin, refuse to listen to the Holy Spirit's promptings, and deny the full authority of God's Word in my life, I am no better than Pilate. My sins nailed Jesus to the cross. But God so loved the world that the story does not stop there! John 3:16 is my redemption song. God's fierce love propels and empowers me to stand up and confront my giants. The Word emboldens me and enriches my life. Reading the Bible gives me confidence to speak truth and verbalize the name of Jesus in my daily life.

There is mercy for us when we fall short of God's glorious standard (Rom. 3:23-24). When we come before the Lord through prayer with sincere, repentant hearts, He forgives us in full. At times, we may fail to obey the Word and represent Jesus well; but because of the cross, Christ's forgiveness is available. God's love is relentless. His mercies are "new every morning; great is [His] faithfulness" (Lam. 3:22-23).

Steps of Faith

- Use the following prayer starter to write out or state a prayer to your Heavenly Father:

  Dear Jesus,

  Forgive me when I . . . Help me with . . . Protect me against . . . Keep my heart . . . Keep my mind . . . Help me to live . . . Show me . . . Teach me . . . Lead me . . . In Jesus' righteous name, amen.

- The disciple Peter and Pontius Pilate both denied Jesus three times on the dark day of Christ's crucifixion. How often do we do the same thing? How often do we sin, let down the Lord, adhere to our own agendas, fail to bear witness, and "deny" our Lord and Savior in these ways? What is the antidote?

33
Selah

Immediately Jesus made the disciples get into the boat and go on ahead of him to

the other side, while he dismissed the crowd. After he had dismissed them, he went

up on a mountainside by himself to pray. Later that night, he was there alone.

Matthew 14:22-23

"WHAT'S WRONG?" MY HUSBAND ASKED me.

I hadn't said anything, but the look in my eyes had given me away. There was so much I could have said. "I feel like I am drowning in a sea of defeat." "Half of my heart is here, while the other half still has hopes, dreams, and aspirations of my own." "Do I truly matter?" "Will I live out my days wiping Play-Doh and crumbs off the kitchen floor?" "Will the sound of children's shows chiming in the background ever go away?"

I was experiencing a typical case of mommy burnout. All of my irrational thinking was adding up and bogging me down. I was feeling overwhelmed, with an underwhelmed soul.

David worked "selahs" into many of his psalms as intentional pauses. Give yourself permission to selah. We, too, must place pauses in our lives and pump the brakes when necessary in order to draw close to God and be rejuvenated through His Word and holy presence. Taking breaks in motherhood enables us to be better moms. It enables us to be more present, more focused, more interactive, and more diligent. Taking a little time to refill frees us up to experience a greater degree of enjoyment in the daily moments of motherhood.

If you are anything like me, you need time away to rejuvenate and recharge. If you are not like me and are okay with momming 24/7/365, then you are a true supermom; and I applaud you for that. But there are different personality types, and some thrive off of taking intermittent sessions to refill.

That day, I was long overdue for a break. It was summertime, and my usual outlets were in vacation mode. Two of my usual outlets include MOPS (Mothers of Preschoolers Organization) and Mother's Day Out. MOPS enables me to fellowship and lean on other mamas. Mother's Day Out gives me a few hours twice a week to do things like grocery shopping by myself, catching up on laundry, listing antiques, and writing the occasional blog.

If you are experiencing feelings of mommy burnout, I want to comfort and assure you that your feelings are normal. You are a good mom. Needing a break to feel like a fully functioning human being every once in a while does not detract any merit from you as a godly mom. If we look at the life of Jesus, we recognize that He often departed from His disciples to be alone and to pray (Matt. 14:13, 22-23).

If we can recognize what we need in order to be better moms, we are doing our entire family a service. Knowing that you need regular breaks is a good thing to realize about yourself. The more we can learn about ourselves to know how we can operate in the very best way, the better. God created you uniquely. Look to your needs so that you can meet the needs of others.

Getting away often means that we can connect with God's heart for us. The first thing I do when I have a chance to be by myself is get in the Word. After that, I try to do something spiritually filling with my time. Sometimes, I read a Christian women's book. Sometimes, I write. Whatever it is that fills your cup, focus on.

Use your time wisely. We may not always have the luxury of going to Starbucks and putting on our headphones, but take advantage of the moments you do have. Maybe it's naptime. Maybe it's after your kids go down for bed. Maybe it's early in the morning. Carve out time for yourself every day and use those minutes wisely. Choose to do things that are spiritually filling and not draining during your precious moments of free time.

Steps of Faith

- Another meaning of "selah" is to stop and take time to listen. Listen for the Lord's voice in your life today. Go to Him in prayer. Pray with praise, repentance, and petition but also take time to pause and listen. Pray something like this:

  Dear Jesus,

  Thank You for the blessing of rest. Thank You for modeling Selah. Help me to follow suit and pursue God intentionally. Holy Spirit, meet me and give me Your peace which surpasses understanding. In Jesus' risen name, amen.

- Make a preemptive plan for what you will do the next time you have some time to yourself. Make a list as a note on your phone. Think about the things that fill your cup.

34
Lord, Have Your Way

If a man or woman living among you in one of the towns the Lord gives you is
found doing evil in the eyes of the Lord your God in violation of his covenant,
and contrary to my command has worshiped other gods, bowing down to
them or to the sun or the moon or the stars in the sky, and this has been
brought to your attention, then you must investigate it thoroughly. If it is true
and it has been proved that this detestable thing has been done in Israel, take
the man or woman who has done this evil deed to your city gate and stone
that person to death.

Deuteronomy 17:2-5

GOD DOES NOT TAKE IDOLATRY lightly. In this day and age, it may not be
the sun, moon, and stars that we are worshiping; but we all weave in and out
of this lane of sin in some way, shape, or form. For many of us, our phones
have become a source of worship. We rely on them like a drug. We depend
on them for comfort, to numb the problems that surround us. Having a
rough day as a mom? Why not scroll through social media until you have
forgotten about it? Feeling down? Why not check your email or texts for a hit
of dopamine?

The problem with these solutions is that they leave no room for God to
step in. We need to seek Jesus through prayer throughout the day. Substituting

our phones for prayer, for more of God Himself, is a form of idolatry that we should be cognizant of and fight against.

For some of us, motherhood itself has become an idol. You might identify as a mom to a point that being a mom comes first—before your marriage, before your relationship with your Heavenly Father. Always remember that before you became a mama, you were and will forever be a daughter of the King. Never forget to praise the One Who made you a mom in the first place. Don't try to use your children to fill a void in your heart that only Jesus is capable of encompassing. Find your identity in Christ alone.

God wants us to water our marriages. As a daughter of Eve, you were created to complete your Adam: to come alongside, nurture, assist in subduing the earth and filling it (Gen. 1:28). You are your spouse's partner, his equal, called to humbly submit. Refuse to let motherhood interfere with your relationship with your husband. Prioritize your marriage by honoring, loving, and faithfully serving your spouse. Marriage is a covenant bond. Treat your marriage with reverence. Cherish it for the holy reflection of Christ's love that it is. Second to our relationship with our Heavenly Father, our marriages should be our most important, prioritized relationship.

Looks can become an idol at any stage in life, including motherhood. We seem to applaud mothers who look like they have stepped out of a magazine right after having a baby. Society often praises moms who can shake their baby fat loose at the drop of a hat. Some moms may be able to snap back immediately after having a baby, while others need a little more time. Whichever end of the pendulum you swing, don't let this become your idol. Our focus should be on pleasing Jesus and serving our families. It is good to feel good about yourself and have confidence in your appearance. But looks are not everything. Don't treat them like they are. Don't place your looks on a pedestal.

In whatever way you struggle, God has the ability to set your priorities straight. He can realign our hearts to be positioned with His own when we seek Jesus through prayer and say, "Lord have Your way."

Steps of Faith

- Pray this prayer:

  Lord,

  Have Your way. Have Your way in my heart. Have Your way in my mind. Have Your way in my actions. Have Your way in my priorities. Have Your way in my home. Intertwine my heart with Your own. Help me to focus on what matters to You most. In motherhood and in life, help me to fixate on loving You fiercely and serving my family faithfully. In Jesus' worthy name, amen.

- Use these Scriptures to fight against various idols in your life:
  - "Devote yourselves to prayer, being watchful and thankful" (Col. 4:2).
  - "And whatever you do, whether in word or deed, do it all in the name of the Lord Jesus, giving thanks to God the Father through him" (Col. 3:17)
  - "Charm is deceitful, and beauty is vain, but a woman who fears the LORD is to be praised" (Prov. 31:30).

35
Rise Up!

When you go to war against your enemies and see horses and chariots and an
army greater than yours, do not be afraid of them, because the Lord your God,
who brought you up out of Egypt, will be with you . . . Do not be fainthearted
or afraid; do not panic or be terrified by them. For the Lord your God is the one
who goes with you to fight for you against your enemies to give you victory.

Deuteronomy 20:1, 3-4

THIS RESOUNDING REASSURANCE WAS GIVEN to the Israelites when they were on the brink of entering into the Promised Land. The Lord assured the Israelites, encouraging them to fight in the name of the Lord and to be strong. God gives us this same mandate and promise today.

When we are given a Heavenly assignment, we are ordained to rise up and fight, to face our giants, to confront our fears. We can do all that God has called us to through Jesus. He gives us assurance. At times, we may fear; but when our confidence wavers, His strength can bridge the gap.

In motherhood, we face giants on a weekly basis. The following are some real-life examples:

- Tackling household chores, even when they are the last thing you want to be doing.

- Attending the birthday party of your child's classmate without knowing a soul.
- Walking into Costco with a baby carrier or multiple toddlers in tow.
- Closing your computer to lead a children's Bible study time.
- Choosing to meal-plan before pursuing whatever else it is you wish to be doing.

Our daily life requires us to listen to the voice of the Lord, to abide in His strength, and to obey, regardless. Regardless of our wants, despite our immediate desires, contrary to our flesh tendencies, opposite of our selfish motives, the Lord desires our hearts. He desires to see purity play out in our daily lives.

When we draw near to the throne of God's grace, we are better able to hear all that He has in store for us. But even when we cannot see, we are called to walk in faithfulness. We have God's Word to rely on.

God equips us to obey. Obedience is a choice. Let the Holy Spirit lead the way. In your heart and through your hands, live for Jesus. Consider His will in all things, for this is "the fear of the Lord, the beginning of knowledge" (Prov. 1:7). Put your head close to God's heart through prayer. Hear the echo of His heartbeat for you throughout the day. Ask Jesus to help you live boldly, undaunted, and unafraid.

In motherhood, our enemies may look a little different than spears, sticks, and stones. Laundry mountains to scale, groceries to gather, homes that need cleaning, meals that need fixing—being the queen bee is no small task! Sticks and stones may break our bones; but the demands of motherhood can overwhelm our minds, threaten our peace, and bog us down when we go at it alone. But through Christ, "we are more than conquerors" (Rom. 8:37). Jesus' presence changes everything. Through the Lord's strength, we can rise up. Invite His presence to envelop your life. Honor your husband (Eph. 5:33), work hard in the home (Titus 2:5), disciple your children (Prov. 22:6). These things are not always convenient or comfortable, but we must fight against the giant of convenience and comfort when hard work and daily diligence is called for.

God desires our obedience. He desires purity to overflow from the wellsprings of our hearts. He desires us to trust in and rely on His strength through the daily battles we face in motherhood. We are called to be brave, obedient, and steadfast. Rise up and fight! And rely on the Lord's presence in your life.

Steps of Faith

- Pray this prayer:

   Dear Jesus,

   Help me to be diligent and focused on serving You and my family. Come alongside me. Give me energy, fortitude, and tenacity to be the best mom that I can be in Your strength. In Jesus' righteous name, amen.

- Reread today's Scripture. Say it out loud.
- State the following. Whisper it as a prayer: "The Lord God of Heaven's armies goes with me. He fights for me. Overwhelming victory is mine through Christ Jesus!"

36
Jesus, Take the Wheel of My Heart

"For I know the plans I have for you," declares the Lord, "plans to prosper you and not to harm you, plans to give you hope and a future. Then you will call on me and come and pray to me, and I will listen to you. You will seek me and find me when you seek me with all your heart.

Jeremiah 29:11-13

"WHY ARE YOU STOPPING, MOMMY?" my little girl, Emma, asked me as we pulled up to the red light.

She did not know why I was slowing down because of her lack of understanding. Her four-year-old perspective had a limited view. I completely understood. I had to stop because of the oncoming traffic intersecting the lane, and the red light legally demanding me to brake.

How often do we do the same thing with God? When the jolly ride of our lives seems to come to a screeching halt, we question God, "Why?" Although we do not always understand the Lord's reasons, we can have confidence in His ways as the Driver of our lives. When we give Jesus the authority to ultimately take the wheel and have full control over our hearts and lives, we can trust and know that His ways are good. Even when we cannot see, we can still have hope and walk in faith knowing that our God has a greater perspective. He knows exactly where He is going and the best way to get there.

So do not fear, Mama. Maybe you feel discouraged, set back in your career, or confused because you did not realize that having kids would be the greatest blessing and biggest challenge of your life, all in one overwhelmingly large bite. I feel for you, Mama. I have been in your shoes. I have shared your joy and laughter but also your tears. God sees you. He has got you in the palm of His hand.

The greatest hope of all is that one day, Jesus will wipe away our every tear. There will be no more pain, death, or sorrow (Rev. 21:4). But even today, we can relax in His love and grace, knowing that the Lord keeps track of our sorrows (Psalm 56:8). Our labor is not in vain. Christ has led us down this motherhood road on purpose, for His kingdom purposes.

So take heart, Mama. Muster up some strength through prayer. Realize that the Lord wants to lead you to the greenest pastures and quietest streams as possible, but it might take some rough terrain and tumultuous trails to get there.

Try to soak in the scenery along the way. Motherhood can be challenging. But if we look for the little things—the sweet/silly things our little ones say; the open mouth kisses; the "I wub yous"; make-believe play; reading books at bedtime; innocent prayers that thank the Lord for things like "Chick-Fil-A," "Costco," "our house," "swimming," "Colorado," and "doing projects with daddy"—then we will be well on our way to adopting hearts of gratitude.

Gratitude is where the joy begins. It is the key that unlocks the door to a spirit overflowing with wisdom, kindness, gentleness, patience, and contentment. These are some places where I struggle. So I am guessing you might at times, too! But through Jesus, we can be overcomers. He can fill the hole in our hearts like nothing else can. Let's make a persistent effort to pray for the Lord to fill us with these things—gratitude, wisdom, kindness, gentleness, patience, and contentment—so that we can be God-honoring examples to the little ones in our lives that matter in such a big way.

Let Jesus take the wheel of your heart and life and trust Him through the rough terrain. Through all things, look to Jesus, the One Who should be in the driver's seat of your life. And if He is not, then, Mama, I think it's time that you get on your hands and knees and pray for the Lord to assume His rightful place as King and Lord of your life.

I am going to lead you in a prayer that invites Jesus to become the Savior of your heart. Let His presence fill you in full so that you can be a beaming blessing to your children and all who know you. Live a changed life through Jesus.

Steps of Faith

- Pray this prayer out loud. Even if you already know Jesus, say this prayer as a reminder to place your faith in Him:

  Dear Jesus,

  Come into my heart and life. Be my Lord, my Savior, and my King. I am officially switching seats and letting You assume your rightful place in the driver's seat of my life. I confess that I am a sinner in need of a Savior. Jesus, forgive me. Jesus, I believe in You. I believe You are fully God and fully man. I believe You died on a wooden cross and rose again. I believe I can do anything and everything You have called me to. In motherhood and in life, be my guide. Thank You, Jesus, for the gift of Your Holy Spirit. Thank You, Jesus, for saving me. In Jesus' almighty name, amen.

- Listen to the song "Jesus Take the Wheel" by Carrie Underwood. Ask Jesus to step into your life and take the wheel of your heart.

37

Above All Else

Love the Lord your God with all your heart and with all your soul and with all your strength. These commandments that I give you today are to be on your hearts. Impress them on your children. Talk about them when you sit at home and when you walk along the road, when you lie down and when you get up. Tie them as symbols on your hands and bind them on your foreheads. Write them on the doorframes of your houses and on your gates.

Deuteronomy 6:5-9

DO YOU EVER FEEL INTIMIDATED by your calling as a mom? I certainly do at times. We are called to rise up and raise an army of Christ's kingdom-shakers and disciple-makers. We have been summoned to work hard in the home (Titus 2:5) and live out our days as Proverbs 31 women. We are commanded to pour ourselves out each and every day, meeting the needs of our little ones. These needs include the basic necessities, such as feeding, clothing, bathing, brushing teeth, and tying shoes. But the realm of these needs has borders that extend beyond the physical and reach the hearts of our children.

Sometimes, I get caught up in all of the busy, and the heart needs of my children get put on the back burner. The basics become too much, and I become exhausted to a point that feeding the souls of my children is the last thing on my to-do list. We must fight to make Christ a priority in our lives, first and foremost; and next in line are our children. Jesus must be our heart's inclination and desire. We must rearrange our lives to seek Jesus first.

When I attended Kanakuk Kamps growing up, they taught us the importance of the "I am third" rule: placing God first, others second, and ourselves third. Prioritizing God first, others second, and ourselves third does not mean meeting our spiritual needs last. Quite the opposite! Living with an "I am third" mindset means we love the Lord God, above all else (Matt. 22:37). We love God through obedience. We love God through time spent in His Word. We love God through prayer and communing with Christ throughout the day. We should focus on the heart needs of our kids because this is what we are called to do. But this does not substitute us meeting with God for ourselves.

The role of mama is a monumental, multifaceted masterpiece. To accomplish it well, we must ask the Holy Spirit to guide our brush strokes. We must listen to His sure, small voice. Sometimes, we may have contrary ideas or preconceived plans as to what our *Starry Night* should look like. But we must value the advice and leadership of our Master, the Lord Jesus Christ. We are apprentices of His Word and will.

God has a special way of using people the world deems insignificant in big ways for Christ's kingdom purposes. You may feel unseen, unheard, undervalued, and unappreciated as a mom. But Christ sees you. He cares about your daily diligence. He has a special portion of love and compassion for you. I truly believe that there is a crown in Heaven for every Christ-believing mama who diligently and faithfully raises up her children in the knowledge and fear of the Lord, teaching them right from wrong and reminding them of God's great love for us.

This Great Love's name is Jesus. He loves you dearly, Mama, for you are His child. He laid down His life for you. There is no greater love. In this same way, we must lay down our lives each day. We must walk in obedience to God's ways, dig into His Word, and strive to plant seeds in our children's hearts whenever and wherever we can. God is with us. God is for us. His grace illuminates the way. His great love is all that we need.

Steps of Faith

- Read through Proverbs 31 and underline the parts that resonate with your heart:

> A wife of noble character who can find? She is worth far more than rubies. Her husband has full confidence in her and lacks nothing of value. She brings him good, not harm, all the days of her life. She selects wool and flax and works with eager hands. She is like the merchant ships, bringing her food from afar. She gets up while it is still night; she provides food for her family and portions for her female servants. She considers a field and buys it; out of her earnings she plants a vineyard. She sets about her work vigorously; her arms are strong for her tasks. She sees that her trading is profitable, and her lamp does not go out at night. In her hand she holds the distaff and grasps the spindle with her fingers. She opens her arms to the poor and extends her hands to the needy. When it snows, she has no fear for her household; for all of them are clothed in scarlet. She makes coverings for her bed; she is clothed in fine linen and purple. Her husband is respected at the city gate, where he takes his seat among the elders of the land. She makes linen garments and sells them, and supplies the merchants with sashes. She is clothed with strength and dignity; she can laugh at the days to come. She speaks with wisdom, and faithful instruction is on her tongue. She watches over the affairs of her household and does not eat the bread of idleness. Her children arise and call her blessed; her husband also, and he praises her: "Many women do noble things, but you surpass them all." Charm is deceptive, and beauty is fleeting; but a woman who fears the Lord is to be praised.

Honor her for all that her hands have done, and let her works bring her praise at the city gate (Prov. 31:10-31).

- Pray this prayer:

  Dear Jesus,

  I pray for Proverbs 31 to come to fruition in my life. Give me wisdom. Help me to walk in grace as Your beloved daughter. In Jesus' precious name, amen.

38
From Bored to Blessed

Therefore, since through God's mercy we have this ministry, we do not lose heart . . . For God, who said, "Let light shine out of darkness," made his light shine in our hearts to give us the light of the knowledge of God's glory displayed in the face of Christ.

2 Corinthians 4:1, 6

DO YOU EVER FEEL BORED being a mom? The day in, day out work is magnanimous, but it can also be monotonous. So how do we fight against our feelings of boredom? How do we alter our lackluster attitude? How can we reach a destination of zeal and delight in what we do? We give it all we've got—100 percent of our effort and energy. Dive in and see how life-giving motherhood can be!

God calls us to live our best lives for Jesus, each and every day. Don't let the sameness of laundry, dishes, and diapers rob your sense of enthusiasm. Get your mind busy and active, fixed and focused on Jesus:

- Cultivate a fruitful prayer life.
- Faithfully read God's Word.
- Meditate on praise and worship music.
- Listen to podcasts that uplift you as a mother and daughter of Christ.

- Read books that encourage you in your walk of faith.
- Invest your time, talent, and treasure in being the best mom that you can be:
- Learn how to be a good cook.
- Read books to your children.
- Tap into your husband's love language.
- Speak to other ladies who can uplift you throughout the week.
- Go through the rhythms of your day with a smile on your face.
- Adopt a joyful and positive attitude.
- Respect your husband's leadership in your home.
- Help out however you can.
- Try to out-serve your spouse.

Be the best mom and wife that you can be, all for God's glory! If we strive for diligence, enthusiasm, a job well done, and joy in our daily lives, we will be far from bored. People will look at our lives and consider us blessed. In this way, we can be lights in this dark world (Matt. 5:14-16).

Shine. Shine bright. Shine bright for Christ. Shine bright for Christ with all of your might. Stay motivated in the mash of the daily grind. Diligently and faithfully serve. Put a smile on your face, remain connected to Jesus, set your hands to the task, and refuse to let boredom override your joy.

Steps of Faith

- Pray this prayer:

> *Dear Jesus,*
> *Thank You for the gift of motherhood and for the sense of purpose and joy it brings to my life. In monotonous moments, remind me of Your goodness and blessings. Thank You for being with me, always. In Jesus' life-giving name, amen.*

- Review the following verses and reflect on how forfeiting over our feelings of boredom for effort and enthusiasm can help us to become better representations of Jesus Christ:

> But we have this treasure in jars of clay to show that this all-surpassing power is from God and not from us. We are hard pressed on every side, but not crushed; perplexed, but not in despair; persecuted, but not abandoned; struck down, but not destroyed. We always carry around in our body the death of Jesus, so that the life of Jesus may also be revealed in our body. For we who are alive are always being given over to death for Jesus' sake, so that his life may also be revealed in our mortal body (2 Cor. 4:7-11).

39
Hope in His Presence

Search me, God, and know my heart; test me and know my anxious thoughts.
See if there is any offensive way in me, and lead me in the way everlasting.

Psalm 139:23-24

WHAT DO YOU PLACE YOUR hope in? We all place our hope in something—whether it's our morning coffee, our husbands, the weekend, time to ourselves (whenever that is), a workout class, or our next meal. What is it that you look forward to with a giddy heart? What do you constantly think about? What do you find yourself drifting off and focusing on? Is it Jesus? Or is it something of this world?

We need to look forward to God's Word as our daily bread. All of our other heart's desires will only bring us emptiness—or fading satisfaction, at best. Yes, some things we look forward to seem shiny and new. But are these things of and from the Lord? That's the question we should be asking ourselves.

Is it wrong to look forward to certain pleasures in life? No! God created us to enjoy life. God loves life. And He put us on this earth to enjoy it. But even more so, He formed us from man's rib and dust for us to help subdue the earth (tame it), and to be fruitful and multiply (both in a literal sense and to make Jesus' name known). We were created to bring God glory. This can be accomplished in more ways than one. Just never forget the main Point—the

One who made a way, the One through which all things are possible (Matt. 19:26). Never forget to set your sights on Jesus.

Weigh your thought life and heart motives against the scales of Christ's righteousness. Filter what it is that you look forward to through the strainer of God's applied truth and the Lord's will for your life. Recognize the deep longing within your soul as a cry for more of Jesus and less of this world. As we live out our days walking on the soil of fallen ground, let us rejoice because of our ultimate hope and joy found in Christ.

The world is a hard, hurting place. It's not supposed to be this way, but the good news is that it won't always be. Christ made a way for you and me to be reunited with our one true Love, Lord, and Savior. It won't be like this for long. So in the meantime, in the here and now, set your eyes on sights above this earth. As an ambassador of Heaven, speak and breathe the Good News into your children and other people's lives.

Salvation is the only thing we have to hold onto. Heaven is the only hope we have to look forward to that is not fleeting. Draw near to the throne of grace each day through God's Word and prayer. Know that there is always and forever a place for you in the presence of Jesus.

Steps of Faith

- Pray this prayer:

    Dear Jesus,

    Help me to place my full heart, hope, and trust in You. God, You alone are my heart's desire. You are all that I need. I come before You with a humble heart and a head bowed low. Keep me within the realm of Your presence, protection, and peace. Guard my heart. Shield my mind from the ways and things of this world so that my heart can focus solely on You, Jesus. Amen.

- What do you need to forfeit today to focus more fully on loving and living for Jesus?

- Review the following verses:
  - "Therefore, since we are surrounded by such a great cloud of witnesses, let us throw off everything that hinders and the sin that so easily entangles. And let us run with perseverance the race marked out for us, fixing our eyes on Jesus, the pioneer and perfecter of faith. For the joy set before him he endured the cross, scorning its shame, and sat down at the right hand of the throne of God" (Heb. 12:1-2).
  - "Since, then, you have been raised with Christ, set your hearts on things above, where Christ is, seated at the right hand of God. Set your minds on things above, not on earthly things. For you died, and your life is now hidden with Christ in God" (Col. 3:1-3).

40
The Meaning of Motherhood

As Jesus and his disciples were on their way, he came to a village where a woman named Martha opened her home to him. She had a sister called Mary, who sat at the Lord's feet listening to what he said. But Martha was distracted by all the preparations that had to be made. She came to him and asked, "Lord, don't you care that my sister has left me to do the work by myself? Tell her to help me!" "Martha, Martha," the Lord answered, "you are worried and upset about many things, but few things are needed—or indeed only one. Mary has chosen what is better, and it will not be taken away from her."

Luke 10:38-42

AS MOMS, IT IS ALL too easy to become distracted and lose sight of what truly matters. We set our sights on things of this world: accomplishments, tidiness, perfection, working out, social media, activities, playdates, preparing meals, laundry, and so much more. While these things are important, we should not let them become viral, conquering every ounce of our time, heart, and attention. So what should we be focused on? What is the constant thing in our lives that we should always be looking toward? His name is Jesus. May we always remember to make a point to come and sit at His feet.

In the daily grind, it is easy to lose sight and difficult to take hold of meaningful moments. It is easy to flow through the motions without being intentional. In our motherhood walks, we should highlight the things that matter to the heart of God. So what are these things? What is meaningful to the Lord? As moms, how can we live out the Gospel each day?

- Laugh!
- Encourage others.
- Embody the ability to not take yourself too seriously. *Seriously.* Have fun with your little ones! Get down on the floor, pretend, and play.
- Show empathy. We must become students of our children, studying their little hearts and minds, in order to be better able to reach their hearts and pierce their minds with the Gospel of Truth.
- Be present in your children's lives. Offer them your full attention and focus. They should not have our complete focus 100 percent of the time but strive to hone in, be present, and pay attention to your children. They need you.
- Love your children and feed them the truth of God's Word. While it can be a challenge to capture your children's fluttering butterfly-like attention, you teach them the meaning of life and what matters most when you read the Bible with them on a consistent basis.
- Be kind. In your actions, words, and tone of voice, strive for gentleness, patience, and God's love.
- Prioritize your relationship with the Lord God, above all else.
- Prioritize your marriage.
- Take your children to church.
- Pray with your little ones. Invite them to pray.

These are just a few things that can set a tone of intentionality in your home. Live out each day for Jesus. Refuse to give into the river of thoughtlessness and ride the current of intentionality instead. It will not come naturally. Being cognizant and intentional never really does. But if we make it a point to stay connected to the Tree of Life, Jesus Christ, each day, then we will be well on our way to living lives of purpose and meaning in motherhood.

Steps of Faith

- Pray this prayer:

  Dear Lord,

  Be with me. Help me to stay mindful today, in tune and in touch with Your heart, God. Give me a spirit of persistence to be faithful in raising up my children according to Your ways. Help me to demonstrate to them the greatness of Your love through the way I live my life. Help me to mother with all my might in Your strength and for Your glory. In Jesus' precious name I pray, amen.

- Reread the bulleted list. What is one way that you can be more intentional as a mama today?
- What is one way that you can be more intentional in your relationship with Jesus today?

41
But God

But because of his great love for us, God, who is rich in mercy, made us alive with Christ even when we were dead in transgressions—it is by grace you have been saved. And God raised us up with Christ and seated us with him in the heavenly realms in Christ Jesus, in order that in the coming ages he might show the incomparable riches of his grace, expressed in his kindness to us in Christ Jesus.

Ephesians 2:4-7

"BUT, MOM . . . " I heard my daughter say, in response to me telling her that she had to eat two more bites of her dinner before she could have a piece of cheddar cheese.

How often do we do the same thing with God? He asks us to do something. He puts a prompting upon our hearts. He opens our eyes to a need that we could meet. *But, God* . . . we mentally whine and complain. We may try to make excuses; but at the end of the day, God's way is always the best way. It is the only way for us to receive His blessings of joy. It is the only way for His favor to rest upon us. It's the only avenue that leads to peace. It is the only way.

Jesus is the only Way (John 14:6). We must comply with His plans. Only through Jesus can we lead holy lives. Apart from Christ, we are lost in a sea of darkness, drowning in our own iniquities and wrongdoings. But God. He made a way. He sent His Son. Jesus died and rose again. We are saved by God's amazing grace, through Christ's redeeming love. This is my resurrection song, my glory story, my only hope.

Jesus Christ, the Son of the Living God is my King. His Spirit is in me. His presence gives me direction. His holiness leads me along righteous paths. His love holds me and carries me through hardships and tumultuous trails.

I love the Lord Jesus with all of my heart. I owe my life to Him. Do you feel the same way? (I am assuming you said yes.) So the next time God asks you to do something, say yes! Say yes to His plans. Say yes to His purposes. Say yes to inconveniences and small sacrifices that ultimately bring Him glory.

Some things the Lord asks for us to do are easy to accomplish. But sometimes, the Lord asks big things of us in order to stretch our faith. But we know that the stretching of our faith produces character and instills in us a sense of steadfast perseverance to pursue the Lord God in all things (James 1:3). *Say yes.*

Saying yes is not always comfortable or easy. Sometimes saying yes can seem like befriending a prickly cactus. But it is what we are called to as Christ-followers. We must go whenever and wherever our Savior leads. Sometimes, we are called to step out of the boat, to brave the wind and the waves. But the good news is that Jesus is right there with us.

Rely on the Holy Spirit inside of you. Depend on what God's Word says. When weighing a decision that is heavy upon your heart, look to God and not yourself. Ephesians 2:8-9 says, "For it is by grace you have been saved, through faith—and this is not from yourselves, it is the gift of God—not by works, so that no one can boast." Refuse to rely on your instinct, or fleeting feelings. Filter your life through the lens of prayer.

The steering wheel of our hearts is slightly tilted to the left. We need God to work through us in every way in order to realign our hearts with His own. Lean into God's Word and pray. The Lord will give you an answer—and His all-consuming peace that comes along with it.

Rest in God's grace. Respond in holiness. Say yes to Jesus.

Steps of Faith

- Pray this prayer:

    Dear Jesus,

    Thank You for the "but God" moments in my life. Thank You for perfectly positioning everything for my good and Your glory. Jesus, I trust You with my current season and future knowing the pages of my life are written to prosper and not harm me, to give me hope and a future because You are a loving, kind God. In Jesus' omnibenevolent name, amen.

- Say yes to God with a cheerful heart and an attitude of gratitude. Second Corinthians 9:7 reminds us, "God loves a cheerful giver."

42
Hidden in Holiness

*"For I know the plans I have for you," declares the Lord, "plans to prosper you
and not to harm you, plans to give you hope and a future. Then you will call
on me and come and pray to me, and I will listen to you. You will seek me and
find me when you seek me with all your heart."*

Jeremiah 29:11-13

THERE'S SOMETHING HOLY IN LIVING a life hidden in Christ. In a day and age that chases after social media accolades, widespread popularity, and fame, it is a humble reminder that God grows us in the hidden, unseen seasons of our lives. Motherhood is one of those seasons.

It might seem like a thankless task; but when we press into providing our presence, the Lord multiplies our heart offering. Like Jesus fed the five thousand using a few fish and loaves of bread, God can use what we have to offer when we give him our all. Giving our all in our homes matters. It matters to our husbands. It matters to our children. It matters to the Lord God.

The world sends the messages, "Hustle"; "Slay"; "Do you anyway." But God's heart is in the hidden, unseen margins of our lives. He grows us in the getting there.

So if you are feeling discouraged at where you are in life, know that God sees you and cares. Jesus spent thirty years of His life leading an ordinary life before He stepped into the light of public ministry. Your behind-the-scenes efforts as a mother, wife, and homemaker matter!

I would love to be able to promise you that God's plans are big and grand. But this is not always the case. Sometimes our lives don't pan out as we had planned. But God's ways are better. He works all things together for the good of those He loves. He works all things together for His glory (Rom. 8:28). This is a truth we can hang our "mama" caps on at the end of the day.

God equips us, builds our character, and develops our perseverance in the hidden years. Every day we are becoming more like the woman God had in mind before time began. Let's humbly, gracefully, and faithfully pursue our roles as mothers and daughters of the King. Let's be so focused on becoming hidden in holiness that pleasing Jesus is the only thing that matters.

Steps of Faith

- Pray this prayer:

  Dear Jesus,

  Thank You for Your model of a life hidden in holiness. I praise You for working all things together for my good. I know You have good plans, and that doesn't always mean "big" plans. Sometimes, Your plans feel hard, but I know that the work I am doing as a mom is holy; and I praise You for that. Please help me be content living a life hidden in Christ. In Jesus' holy name, amen.

- Read the entirety of Jeremiah 29 and recognize how the hope God provided wouldn't unfold until seventy years later. God's plans are always good and are always for His glory and not our own. His promises in our lives might not always happen immediately, but we can have faith through our desert years knowing that God sees us and is always working things together for our good.

43
Confidence—Just Ask!

Which of you, if your son asks for bread, will give him a stone? Or if he asks
for a fish, will give him a snake? If you, then, though you are evil, know how
to give good gifts to your children, how much more will your Father in heaven
give good gifts to those who ask him! So in everything, do to others what you
would have them do to you, for this sums up the Law and the Prophets.

Matthew 7:9-12

WHAT MAKES YOU INSECURE AS a mom? Is it your graying hair, your
weight, your acne, your aging skin, your lack of a paycheck? What is it that
bothers you and makes you feel insufficient? Christ can fill the gaps of the
things we lack. He can replace our feelings of insufficiency with His sufficient
truth that says we are chosen (1 Peter 2:9), worth far more than rubies (Prov.
3:15), forgiven (2 Cor. 12:9), and beautiful because of our hearts (1 Sam. 16:7).

Seek wisdom, seek truth, seek for God's love to overflow out of you. Grace
the lives of others because of your love for the Lord. Live from the truth that
says you are "a chosen . . . royal priesthood," created to praise Jesus (1 Peter
2:9). Declare His name over your life. Absorb the wisdom of the Word. Come
and sit at the feet of Jesus. Find confidence in God's grace. Plant your feet on
the solid rock of God's truth in your life. Place your hope in Heaven. Live like
only Jesus is watching.

When we find solace in Christ's presence, we create a model for our children to take note of. They are definitely taking notes. I want my children to look back and remember that they had a mother who loved Jesus, a mother who lived a life of sold-out devotion to the Lord, a mother who was deeply rooted in the Word, a mother who was brave for God, a mother who followed the Holy Spirit's promptings in her life, a mother whose confidence was found in Christ alone.

God keeps His promises. He is faithful, even when we are not. Even when our wayward hearts cause us to trip and stumble because of sin, God's Word never fails (Luke 1:37). If we know and believe in this truth, then we should have rays of beaming confidence in Christ exuding from our lives. Jesus is going to follow through. God's grace covers our wayward hearts. His plans are good. His promises stand true. We have hope and assurance because of Jesus.

If you lack confidence, ask God to give you some! If you lack wisdom, ask for Jesus to provide (James 1:5)! If you lack joy, ask God to envelop your life with his illuminating grace. God is in the business of giving. If we continue to ask, we are likely to receive (Matt. 7:7-8). The Lord withholds no good thing from those He loves, whose walk is blameless (Psalm 84:11). We all have insecurities; but when we look at what truly matters in this life, we can be reassured that the presence of Jesus in our lives is greater than all of these things. We have hope in our hearts because of the eternal life we are guaranteed through Christ. Live from this truth. You are chosen. You are royal. You are beautiful. Your heart is all that God sees.

Steps of Faith

- Pray this prayer:

  Lord Jesus,
  Thank You for being my daily bread. Give me Your confidence.
  Give me wisdom from Your Word. Help me to live a life of

*confidence and contagious joy because of my hope that is
ultimately found in You. In Jesus' holy name, amen.*

- Reflect on the following verses. Let your heart resonate with
  the fact that Jesus loves you. He goes before you. His promises
  stand true.
  - "Trust in the LORD with all your heart and lean not on your
    own understanding; in all your ways submit to him, and he
    will make your paths straight" (Prov. 3:5-6).
  - "Not one of all the LORD's GOOD promises to Israel failed;
    every one was fulfilled" (Josh. 21:45).
  - "'Ask and it will be given to you; seek and you will find;
    knock and the door will be opened to you. For everyone
    who asks receives; the one who seeks finds; and to the one
    who knocks, the door will be opened'" (Matt. 7:7-8).
- Write out a prayer in your journal or as a note on your phone.
  Ask God to grace your life with confidence in Christ and wisdom
  from the Word.

44
Heart Inventory Check

I pray that the eyes of your heart may be enlightened in order that you may know the hope to which he has called you, the riches of his glorious inheritance in his holy people.

Ephesians 1:18

I BUY AND SELL ANTIQUE decorative items to make a little extra income for my family. When antique shopping, I have to weed through massive quantities of junk in order to find "the diamond in the rough." So it is with our spiritual lives. God sorts through the conditions of our hearts in order to find what He is so avidly searching for: a reflection of His own heart. He will continue sorting through the Beanie Babies and vintage Coca-Cola signs because God's pursuit of our hearts doesn't skip a beat.

When antique shopping, there are acute standards that I look for in potential inventory items:

- Quality
- Authenticity
- Desirability
- Condition
- Aesthetics

We can apply these same standards to the conditions of our hearts:

- Quality: one tool of measurement for the quality of our hearts is accountability. This can be accomplished through counseling or a Christian accountability partner. Another sand-sifter that we can use to sort out the impurities of our lives is prayer. With a genuine, humble heart, plead for the Lord to reveal any offensive way in you.
- Authenticity: cultivate an authentic, thriving relationship with the Lord through time spent faithfully in God's Word.
- Desirability: people should notice something different about our lives. Contagious joy, eternal hope, unwavering faith: Let's be "the salt of the earth" (Matt. 5:13).
- Condition: the conditions of our hearts should be transparent and become apparent through how we are demonstrating Jesus' greatest commandments to "'Love the Lord your God with all your heart and with all your soul and with all your mind' and 'Love your neighbor as yourself'" (Matt. 22:37-39).
- Aesthetics: is there ripe fruit evident in your life? Love, joy, peace, patience, kindness, goodness, faithfulness, gentleness, and self-control—these are the fruits of the Spirit (Gal. 5:22-23). The Bible says, "By their fruit you will recognize them. Do people pick grapes from thornbushes, or figs from thistles?" (Matt. 7:16). The overflow of our hearts is evident by the way we live our lives. The words we say, the choices we make, and our attitudes represent the condition of our spirits.

The Lord desires to instill wisdom from His Word, godly character, the fruits of the Spirit, and the attributes of the Proverbs 31 woman inside of us all. When we fall short of God's perfect standard, act impulsively, and sin,

God offers us His grace. Because of the cross, we can be forgiven. Live a life of freedom, inspired by the fact that Jesus gave it all.

Let us be mindful of our habits and heart motivations. May everything we do and pursue praise the Lord. May the inventory of our hearts align with God's vision and plan for our lives.

God wants us to become more like Him. Let's stock the shelves of our hearts with attributes that are pleasing and precious in His sight. Through God's Word, accountability, prayer, and continual pursuit of Christ, may we live our lives emboldened to look a little more like Jesus each day.

Steps of Faith

- Pray this prayer:

  Dear Jesus,

  Thank You for Your hand over my heart. Thank You for pruning me, pursuing me, and purifying my life according to Your Word. I pray that I would fully rely on Your wisdom in all things. Teach me to listen. Teach me to abide in Your presence. Teach me to walk in Your ways. In Jesus' almighty name, amen.

- Prayer is a precious, beautiful thing. But often, we don't take the time to stop talking, humble our hearts, and listen. So lean in and listen today. Listen throughout the day.

- The Greek word for Christian is *christianos*, which derives from two Greek words, *christos* and *tianos,* which translate respectively to "anointed" and "little." So the word "Christian" literally means, "little anointed one." Read Matthew 5 today and take note of the ways Jesus calls us to live according to a higher standard. By studying the life and character of Christ, we can learn how to stock the shelves of our hearts with attributes that are precious and praiseworthy in His sight.

45
Vessels

But we have this treasure in jars of clay to show that this all-surpassing power
is from God and not from us. We are hard pressed on every side, but not
crushed; perplexed, but not in despair; persecuted, but not abandoned;
struck down, but not destroyed.

2 Corinthians 4:7-9

POTTERY IS A CERAMIC WARE that is fired in a kiln at high temperatures to remove all excess water from the clay. Pottery comes in all different shapes and sizes and has an array of different purposes and functions. But to be considered pottery, the medium used has to contain clay when formed. Clay is composed of silica, magnesia or alumina—or both—and water. Clay demonstrates plastic properties. It is malleable. It is moldable. It can be used to create different shapes and sizes of vessels.

In the same way that clay exhibits plastic properties, we are to demonstrate the ability to be flexible and conform to God's image and plan for our lives. As the body of Christ, our calling might look a little different than our friends', but that is the beauty of being uniquely formed. God created us in His image with certain attributes that contribute to our roles as mothers, wives, and daughters of Christ.

The purpose of a vessel is to hold water. I find it ironic that the process of creating an earthenware vessel constitutes removing the water from the clay through the process of firing, yet pottery was essentially made to hold liquid. We were made to house the Holy Spirit inside of us, yet we are sinful beings. Only through the firing process, the saving grace and unfailing mercy of God, is this possible.

When we were grafted into the family of Christ through salvation, God began to mold, shape, and form us into His image. He continues to mold and shape us throughout the course of our lives. He never stops firing the sin out of us. It is a purification process that is achieved through heat and pressure, hardship and trials, disobedience and repentance.

Sometimes, the heat and pressures of life feel like being fired in a pottery kiln. When calamity strikes and we do not know why, we can have hope through the hard moments to endure because Christ endured on our behalf. The ultimate battle for our souls has already been won. We have a reason for promising peace, confident hope, and lasting joy because of the cross.

Like pottery, we will feel the high temperatures of firing throughout the course of our lives. Through it all, we must draw near to Jesus, bring God glory, exude confident hope, and transpire testimonies of God's faithfulness to our children and all we know.

God has His hand on our children's hearts. He is the Sculptor of their lives. This should come as a relief to us because although we are called to teach our children about Jesus, the Holy Spirit is ultimately the One Who calls them home.

We must share our testimonies of how God enables us to endure the heat and trials of life. Pottery is an artform that should be displayed. Don't hide all that God has done in your life. Put it on a shelf for the world to see, admire, and be inspired. Make sure that shelf is low enough for your children to view and grasp the beauty and power of your brilliant testimony.

Only through Christ can we come out glazed, perfected, and beautiful on the other side. Trials stretch our faith and make it firm. Hardships present high temperatures that solidify our faith in Christ. Tribulations test our faith to produce perseverance to finish the race. James encourages us, "Consider it pure joy, my brothers and sisters, whenever you face trials of many kinds, because you know that the testing of your faith produces perseverance. Let perseverance finish its work so that you may be mature and complete, not lacking anything" (James 1:2-4).

If you have ever been to a pottery painting place, you know that the colors you paint transform and become much more vibrant, glossy, and glazed after the firing process. So it is with our trials in life. Only by clinging to the cross through it all can we be made beautiful. Our scars can become colorful brushstrokes that exude vibrant shades when we allow Christ to perfect our faith.

When you walk through a difficult time in life, instead of blaming God, proclaim His holy name. Cry out to Jesus. Cling tightly to His hand through his truth and promises. His purposes are for us. Sometimes the unfolding process is painful; but ultimately, God is going to have His way in our hearts and lives. We will make it to the peaceful streams and gentle waters in the Lord's perfect timing.

When we hold onto our faith and trust in Jesus through our "shadow of death" (Psalm 23:4) moments, we will reach a better understanding of the Lord's goodness. He will never leave or forsake us (Heb. 13:5). His promises and plans for our lives are ultimately good. We can rest on this truth and face the kiln with confidence, knowing that there is a purpose behind the pain that presents itself in our lives.

Christ gives us the strength to endure. We will not shatter; we will not be destroyed. We will experience pain; but our faith will be perfected in the process, and we will come out beautiful on the other side.

Steps of Faith

- Pray the following in your heart or out loud:

    Dear Jesus,
    Thank You for Your ultimate goodness, that You are the Potter
    in my life. You know the exact temperatures I need to become

pottery, and You monitor those temperatures closely. Lord, I know that You will never allow my faith to be shattered but will always find a way to bring me back to You and Your heart. Thank You for Your love and kindness. In Jesus' sovereign name I pray, amen.

46
What Are Your Thoughts?

Do not conform to the pattern of this world, but be transformed by the
renewing of your mind. Then you will be able to test and approve what God's
will is—his good, pleasing and perfect will.

Romans 12:2

WHAT IS YOUR THOUGHT LIFE like? When you hear that question, what comes to mind? Do the ripe fruits of the Holy Spirit appear? Or does discord and dysfunction creep in? Are you thinking about Jesus, or fixating on something else? Are your thought patterns pleasing to the Lord? Are you constantly considering Jesus' point of view? These are questions we must ask ourselves to get to the heart of the matter.

Scripture tells us that "the fear of the Lord is the beginning of knowledge" (Prov 1:7). I have heard it said that the fear of the Lord is placing God's opinion first on the forefront of your mind all of the time.

This is an area where I struggle. My mind is not murky, mucky, or muddy, by any means; but sometimes, my thoughts are not parked where they should be. I focus on things of this world that are right in front of me before considering God's thoughts. We should approach each day with a Heaven mindset. "Will this matter in light of eternity?" is a question we should ask ourselves before devoting too much time, focus, and heart energy on the matter.

When I open up my Bible, I notice that the Israelites also had wandering hearts. In the book of Judges, it is apparent that they placed other gods before the Lord. They committed idolatry in worshiping the gods of the Canaanites, Hittites, Amorites, Perizzites, Hivites, and Jebusites (Judg. 3:5-6). They intermarried with these foreign nations; and as a result, their influence tainted the Israelites' judgment and sound thinking. What they knew to be true was overridden because their intake and surroundings were not of the Lord.

We must immerse our lives in living for Christ. We must conform our thought patterns to loving and praising God. We must resituate our surroundings and influences to be set on serving the Lord of Heaven's armies.

Jesus wants us to be brave. He calls us out of the boat to face the wind and the waves. Evaluate your heart and be honest with yourself. Is your thought life pleasing to Jesus? He cares. He truly cares about the conditions of your heart. So in what way can we reposition our minds to focus on all that is "true . . . noble . . . right . . . pure . . . lovely . . . admirable . . . excellent or praiseworthy" (Phil. 4:8)?

- Read God's Word. I've said it before, but I'll say it again! God's Word is the best weapon we have to fight against spiritual warfare in our lives.
- Monitor your intake. What are you reading? What kind of music are you listening to? What shows have you been watching lately? Our intake greatly affects our spiritual well-being.
- Pray. Confess ugly, ungodly thoughts to Jesus. Ask for His forgiveness. Seek His help in changing your thought patterns through prayer.
- Ask someone you know and love to pray for you.

The next time you find your thoughts wandering from where they should be, remind your heart, *"This is where Jesus resides!"* We are temples of the Holy

Spirit. The God of the universe is alive in us! He gives us the power to conquer ungodly thoughts and attitudes and triumph over evil in our lives.

Sometimes, ungodly thought patterns begin to cycle in our minds and fill up the room of our hearts like a smoker's exhale. Declare to yourself, "This is a non-smoking zone!" Ask Jesus to step in and unfog your mind. Ask the Lord to purify the conditions of your heart, to give you a fresh slate, a newly plowed field, a garden of grace and gratitude. Plant God's Word in your heart. Replace all of the yuck with Jesus' life-giving grace, peace, promises, and presence. Your life will be changed when you do.

Steps of Faith

- Pray this prayer:

  Dear Lord,

  Have Your way. Have Your way in my heart and my life. Jesus, I know that You want all of me: my heart, my soul, my mind, and my strength to reflect Your truth. Position my thoughts to glorify You. In Jesus' sanctified name, amen.

- For the next few days, listen to Christian music only. This might seem extreme, but give it a try. Take note of the benefits it presents to the health of your heart and your relationship with Christ.

47
Well-Watered Mama

"But blessed is the one who trusts in the Lord, whose confidence is in him. They will be like a tree planted by the water that sends out its roots by the stream. It does not fear when heat comes; its leaves are always green. It has no worries in a year of drought and never fails to bear fruit."

Jeremiah 17:7-8

I REMEMBER HIKING WITH MY husband in the beautiful countryside of Arkansas. We were relative newlyweds in our pre-kid era. My husband, Dave, told me to ration my water as best as I could—as in, don't drink very much. We had only the amount of water that we could carry on our backs. I tried to listen; but being slightly ignorant and thirsty, I quickly consumed all of my water. I struggled with thirst the remainder of the hike. My kind, loving husband gracefully shared some of his water supply with me, but it was not quite enough to be truly satisfied.

Being thirsty is a real human problem, but have you ever been spiritually thirsty? The struggle is real and manifests itself in different ways. Sometimes, we struggle with ignorance to the fact that we need Jesus. We bring the thirst upon ourselves. In the form of pursuing other mini gods to satisfy our soul longings, we deny what it is that our hearts truly need. We pursue status, portraying a picture-perfect lifestyle on social media, chasing after influence, and striving to obtain bodies that match the sleek figures displayed on magazines. We try to elevate ourselves in terms of performance and outward appearance. We try to achieve and numb ourselves to what it is we crave through means of entertainment and our phones.

But we need to remember the truth: all of these things will leave us feeling desperately thirsty. The precursor verses to today's verse, Jeremiah 17:5-6, states, "'Cursed is the one who trusts in man, who draws strength from mere flesh and whose heart turns away from the Lord. That person will be like a bush in the wastelands; they will not see prosperity when it comes. They will dwell in the parched places of the desert, in a salt land where no one lives.'"

Our number one desire in life must be Jesus. And if it is not, may we recognize this and pinpoint the fact that what our hearts truly crave is the presence of the living God in our lives. All of the other things we seek will only draw up an empty bucket from a dry well.

We need to get back to our first Love. His name is Jesus Christ. We are His beloved, the ones that He gave His life for. Be like the well-watered woman in the Bible who found the source of Living Water. Jesus met her at her point of need, at the well. He saw through her—her weaknesses, her shame, her desperation, her sins, and her cry for help. He sees you, too, Mama.

Come to the well. Recognize what it is you so avidly search for as the Source of where Living Water freely flows. The presence of Jesus is ours to behold. Chase after God's heart and Jesus' plans for you each day. Fill your cup through God's Word and prayer. We need Jesus now more than ever, more than anything, to satisfy the desperate cries of our mama souls. Recognize what it is that you truly long for: the Living Water that derives from Jesus Christ. Let Him quench your thirst. Accept the grace Jesus has for you.

Steps of Faith

- Pray this prayer:

    Dear Jesus,

    Fill me today. My heart longs for You. My soul cries out in desperation. Quench my thirst by drawing near to me, as I draw near to You. In Jesus' soul-satisfying name, amen.

- What is it that you have been chasing after lately? Go to the Lord in prayer and confess what you have been searching and seeking, other than Christ. Talk to Jesus about it. Ask Him to fill your cup and satisfy your desperate need for more of His presence in your daily life.

- Meditate on the following verse: "Serve only the LORD your God and fear him alone. Obey his commands, listen to his voice, and cling to him" (Deut. 13:4).

48
Shine Bright

"So may all your enemies perish, Lord! But may all who love you be like the sun when it rises in its strength."

Judges 5:31

SHINE BRIGHT! THIS IS OUR sole purpose in life. We are lights of the world, cities on a hill (Matt. 5:14). We are called to exude radiant beams of Christ's hope and promises into the darkness and pitch-black night. I am certain that you have heard this before. But what does this actually look like in our daily lives? How can we literally, spiritually, and tangibly shine for Jesus each day?

- Speak words that shine the light. Let your words be grace-filled and edifying to all who hear. Use your words to lift others up, not to tear down or defame. Avoid the gray areas of gossip.
- Do deeds that shine for Jesus. Shining can be in the small things. Little acts of generosity and courage are acutely noticed by our Heavenly Father.
- Shine God's light into your family. Your home is your mission field! We are called to "go and make disciples of all nations" (Matt. 28:19), yes, indeed. But first and foremost, consider the potential eternal impact you could have on your children's hearts and in your husband's life. You have a salient part to play. Shine bright!

- Reach out to the lost and the hurting. Sponsor a child who is impoverished and in need of Jesus' love. Talk to your kids about this endeavor.

- Reach out to other mothers who are hurting, searching, and unknowingly seeking Jesus. Think of a mama in your life who does not know the Lord. Befriend that mama, even when it feels awkward, uncomfortable, or unsolicited. Befriend her. Establish a relationship with her and lead her to Jesus in the best way that you know how. Shine into the darkness—the lives of the lost and broken.

- Share your testimony. Our testimonies are our most powerful tools of evangelism. There is resurrection power, God-given authority, and Christ-infused boldness in the words of our testimonies breathed into other people's lives. The Holy Spirit has a way of using our testimonies for His kingdom purposes to change hearts. Don't underestimate the power of your sharing and opening up your heart to other women through unveiling your former weaknesses, tribulations, and struggles and highlighting how Jesus uplifted you through it all. Speak the name of Jesus by sharing your testimony.

Meet the needs of those who do not know Jesus. Plain and simple. Talk about Jesus. Love like Jesus. Live and befriend sinners, like Jesus. We need close Christian friends, but we are also called to reach out and be branches that connect and lead others to the source of our fruit. Branch out to those who are disconnected, lost in darkness.

Be fruitful through love. Be fruitful through grace. Be generous. Be kind. Turn the other cheek. Look around for those in need and bring them along with you. Share your light. It provides warmth and sight, reveals perils in life, and shows us the way to eternal life through Jesus.

We are reflections of God's glory and goodness. Live boldly for Christ, undaunted and unashamed. Declare His name through the way you live your life. Don't be shy to speak the name of Jesus into lost people's lives. Share your testimony. *Shine brightly.*

Steps of Faith

- Pray this prayer:

  Dear Jesus,

  Give me Christ-infused boldness and the essence of God's love to speak Your truth into lost people's lives. Show me how to establish connections and relationships with those people, creating a bridge that the Holy Spirit can cross over and enter into their hearts. In Jesus' lovely name, amen.

- Read the Message version of Matthew 5:14-16 and prayerfully consider what this could look like in your life:

  "Here's another way to put it: You're here to be light, bringing out the God-colors in the world. God is not a secret to be kept. We're going public with this, as public as a city on a hill. If I make you light-bearers, you don't think I'm going to hide you under a bucket, do you? I'm putting you on a light stand. Now that I've put you there on a hilltop, on a light stand—shine! Keep open house; be generous with your lives. By opening up to others, you'll prompt people to open up with God, this generous Father in heaven."

49
leave a legacy

I have fought the good fight, I have finished the race, I have kept the faith.
Now there is in store for me the crown of righteousness, which the Lord, the
righteous Judge, will award to me on that day—and not only to me, but also
to all who have longed for his appearing.

2 Timothy 4:7-8

AT THE END OF MY days, I want the good Lord to look at me and confidently say, "'Well done, my good and faithful servant'" (Matt. 25:21). Like Paul, when my life nears its end, I want to look back and be able to honestly say, "I have fought the good fight, I have finished the race, I have kept the faith" (2 Tim. 4:7). In other words, "I have fought for Christ to be the Center of my life. I have impacted the lives of others in Jesus' name. I have lived out my days faithfully and persistently pursuing Jesus."

What fight are you fighting? Are you fighting the good fight? Or something that is of a lesser caliber? Everyone is fighting for something.

Are you fighting for Christ, or are you fighting for yourself? Are you fighting to become famous, or are you fighting to make Christ's name known? Are you fighting for dominance in your home, or are you fighting for Christ to be the ultimate Leadership in your household? Are you fighting for control over your children, or are you fighting for God to have control over their hearts? Are you fighting to be present and consistent in your children's lives, or are you living for yourself and letting your attention wander?

What legacy is it that you are leaving? Is it that of grace through faith? This is the formula for salvation (Eph. 2:8). Forever with the Lord in eternity is ours to behold through Christ Jesus. Are you imparting the knowledge of this truth into your children's lives?

Are you rising up to receive the crown of righteousness Paul speaks of? We do this by making Christ's name known. We do this through consistently reviewing God's Word and through persistent prayer. We do this by focusing on matters of eternity. We do this through acts of love, kindness, and generosity.

Speak the name of Jesus in your heart and in your home. Mention Him to other moms in your life. Give God glory and reflect on His goodness. Through the trials and hardships you encounter, have steadfast peace in God's promises. Buoy your hope to Jesus and remain connected to circumstance-surpassing joy. Let God be your lighthouse and be drawn into a place of safety and warmth, an oasis away from life's rough waters, through His holy presence.

We fail when we take our eyes off Jesus. But there is grace when we fail. We all fall short of God's glorious standard (Rom. 3:23). Still we must ask ourselves the question, "Am I living life in reflection of the fact that God is my everything?"

The first and greatest commandment we have been given is to "'love the Lord your God with all your heart and with all your soul and with all your mind,'" and "'the second is like it: *Love your neighbor as yourself*'" (Matt. 22:36-39). The fact that the Bible states, "The second is like it" implies that when we love our neighbors, we are loving the Lord God Himself.

Our neighbors are anyone and everyone within our sphere of influence. The people closest to this bull's-eye are our children and husband. Are you loving them like you love yourself? This kind of love leaves a legacy.

Love is strong like water. It takes multiple forms. At times, it is a rushing river flooding in, full of emotion and endorphin-infused energy. At other moments in life, it is like the sea. Its energy comes in waves that are patterned and predictable. This predictability gives us confident assurance and peace. Still at other times, love is like the frozen arctic tundra, beneath which sea creatures lie. The energy is frozen and fixed. But perhaps it is even stronger than ever, immovable, unbreakable, and unchanging. Love ebbs and flows throughout the course of our lives, but God's love is constant. His grace covers us. His faithfulness remains true.

Are you exuding this kind of Heavenly, fixed, undaunted love to your neighbors—your children? Or are you letting your emotions control you? At times, loving our neighbors is an untidy task. It looks like giving your child a spanking, imparting godly wisdom, redirecting, and giving a big hug and an "I love you" afterward. It looks like pushing your child on a swing, playing trains, devoting your full focus on their little heart needs, and not drifting off on your phone. It looks like reading that bedraggled children's Bible one more time, even though it feels repetitive. In all of these instances, ask the Holy Spirit to step in. Ask Him to be your steady Strength. Ask for the Lord's faithfulness to override your faithlessness (2 Tim. 2:13).

Sometimes, we might feel like our efforts in motherhood go unnoticed. Remain faithful to the task, anyway. God notices, even when no one else does. Rest on this solid rock of truth. God cares about the legacy of love and faithfulness you are leaving for your children. Some days, we might fail; but God remains faithful, even when we are not.

Steps of Faith

- Pray this prayer:

  Dear Jesus,
  Thank You for Your abundant love and forever faithfulness.
  Help me to live a diligent life as a mom and follower of Christ.

Situate the posture of my heart and attitude to reflect Your image in all I do. As I pursue You and Your heart, strengthen my faith and enhance the godly attributes of my character. Lord, use me as a vessel in my home. In Jesus' sanctified name, amen.

- Think of someone who was in your life that you loved who has passed away. Think of things they did that inspired you and ways they made you feel special and loved. Try to emulate these things and breathe the same kind of love and care into your children's lives.

50
Refract the light

For this reason, ever since I heard about your faith in the Lord Jesus and your love for all God's people, I have not stopped giving thanks for you, remembering you in my prayers. I keep asking that the God of our Lord Jesus Christ, the glorious Father, may give you the Spirit of wisdom and revelation, so that you may know him better. I pray that the eyes of your heart may be enlightened in order that you may know the hope to which he has called you, the riches of his glorious inheritance in his holy people.

Ephesians 1:15-18

THIS IS MY PRAYER FOR you! These verses are part of a letter Paul wrote to encourage and inspire the church of Ephesus to chase after Jesus, wholeheartedly. I encourage you to do the same. Proclaim His holy name! In your home and everywhere you go, be love. Speak love. Spread the name of Jesus.

Talk about Jesus with your children. Pray with them. Invite them to pray. Use your testimony to spur on other mothers for Jesus. Lace your day with godly checkpoints like prayer, reading your Bible, listening to Christian music, acknowledging His holy presence, counting your blessings, and listening for the Holy Spirit.

Let Jesus in. Allow Christ to fill up your home and your heart. Use the gifts God has given you as a woman and daughter of Christ to mother with all your might. In Jesus, for Jesus, and through Jesus, be the best mom that you can be, all for your Heavenly Father's glory.

Open the eyes of your heart. Christ wants to do an earth-quaking, mountain-moving, community-shaking, tribe-transforming work in you as a mother and daughter of the King. Live your best life for Jesus. Allow Him to sanctify the conditions of your heart.

There is power in the name of Jesus. Believe in this truth. Live from this truth. Pray from this truth. Lavish this truth upon the little lives in front of you. Thrive where you are planted, and make Jesus' name known.

Have grace for yourself in moments of weakness and desperation. Cry out to Jesus. He wants to take you by the hand and never let you go. In the busy parking lot of this world, allow God to lead you and keep you forever safe within His loving grasp.

I remember when my two-year-old son, Josiah, broke his leg. It just about broke my heart! As much as it hurts you to stand by and witness your children experience physical pain, the Lord has compassion and empathy for us when we struggle. He wants to help us. He wants to see us healed and set free from our suffering, sorrow, and setbacks. He wants to watch us gracefully swim, thriving in our roles as mothers. But this is a choice we must make for ourselves. *Choose Jesus.* We can't do it by ourselves. Trying to swim in our own strength will surely cause us to sink. Depend on Christ as your Lifeline, your Saving Grace.

The world is a hard, hurting place. We need the Lord's presence to envelop us like a holy sanctuary. We need His sure, small voice to calm our anxious hearts. We need his Holy Spirit to illuminate our lives. We need His grace to cover us, and His joy to fill us in full. We need the peace of His presence to encapsulate our worried minds. We need His goodness and mercy to overflow from the wellsprings of our hearts. All of this can be accomplished because of the cross. Because of what Jesus did for you and me, we can live forever set free. His ultimate sacrifice opened doors for us to walk through to experience the rapture of living within the freedom boundaries of God's love and grace.

We live in a world between two gardens, the Garden of Eden and the Garden of Christ's Kingdom on Earth that He will establish one glorious day. Until then, let us live within the margin of possibility. May our lives refract the light of Christ in unique and Heavenly ways because of the ultimate hope we have in eternity. Let your life sing a love song to the Lord in light of the fact that one beautiful day, we will be reunited with our one true Love, Lord, and Savior.

Let each moment of motherhood praise the Lord. With every boo-boo kissed, every popsicle passed out, every small, salty tear wiped away, every spout of luminous laughter shared, every "I love you" stated, every seat belt buckled, every diaper changed, every after-school snack and dinner made, every storybook read, every "Jesus loves you" ever said, put a smile on Jesus' face.

Believe it or not, you will be needed less and less. But until then, in the here and now of sticky fingers, mac and cheese, and "I wub you's," honor the Lord in the little things. Until that beautiful, glorious day when you get to look upon your Heavenly Father's loving gaze, let every breath you take praise the Lord.

Steps of Faith

- Pray the following. Let the words sink down deep into your soul and lead you to live a changed life:

> *Dear Jesus,*
>
> *Thank You for loving me fiercely. Help me to lavish Your great love upon my children and family. Help me to honor You through motherhood. Equip me to do Your will and to live faithfully for You alone, Jesus. Thank You for the gift of being a mom. Thank You for the blessings of my children. Aid me in sending them off like flaming arrows into this dark world. Help me to be a reflection of Your light, an example of Your great love. Come alongside me on this motherhood journey. Be my*

Guiding Light and Source of strength. I need You, Jesus. Thank You for saving me. In the perfect, powerful, praiseworthy name of Jesus I pray, amen.

- Read the following definition of grace: "Grace is God's undeserved favor, and I like to say it is also God's power coming to us freely to help us do with ease what we could never do on our own with any amount of struggle and effort."[4]

- **Rest** in God's unmerited favor today and mother in honor of the truth that Christ will forever and always meet you halfway. Give it your all and trust in the Lord with the rest. Have peace in Christ's strength. Have hope in the Lord's provision. Have mercy for yourself and others. Have faith in the knowledge of God's goodness. Rely on the realization of his redemptive, hope-filled plans for your future (Jer. 29:11).

- **Pursue** Christ's heart, as you float in the freedom power of God's amazing grace. Always remember that "it is by *grace* you have been *saved*"—eternally, completely, forever and always, once and for all. You have been set free, and "this is not from yourselves" (Eph. 2:8, emphasis mine).

- **Praise** God for His grace that adorns your head like a crown of woven wildflowers. Praise Jesus for His blood poured out that has appointed you as His holy, treasured, beloved possession. Never forget: you have been called, were created, have been ordained by the anointing blood of Jesus to declare the praises of the Lord's glorious light and unconditional love (1 Peter 2:9).

- **Rest** in God's love. **Pursue** the Lord's plans and purposes. **Praise** Jesus with all of your heart, mind, soul and strength. This is the essence of grace!

---

4   Joyce Meyer, *Overcoming Every Problem* (New York: FaithWords, 2023), 72.

Did this devotional encourage, refresh, or draw you closer to Jesus in some way? If so, I would love to hear about it! Reviews help readers find the right books to fit their needs. Please consider leaving a review.

About Alex

ALEXANDRA JENSEN—"ALEX," AS HER FRIENDS call her—resides in Tulsa, Oklahoma. She is married to her husband, Dave, and they have three beautiful, energetic kids. Emma is four; Josiah is three; and Madison is one. Alex is a member and Steering team leader of the organization MomCo., where she has developed deeply rooted friendships. Alex loves the Lord and studying His Word daily. She enjoys reading, blogging, antique shopping, jogging, jewelry making, the beach, queso, a good Starbucks, and all things fun!

Stay in Touch

For weekly encouragement subscribe to Alex's blog:

www.alexandrajensen.org

Follow her on social media:

Facebook.com/authoralexandrajensen

Instagram @authoralexandrajensen

Pinterest @authoralexandrajensen

Please send Alex an email if you would like to schedule her as a speaker or podcast guest.

Email: alexandrajensen91@gmail.com

Bibliography

Barrett, Brianna. "Let Go and Let God." *A Place of Grace for Moms of Littles*. Ambassador International, 2024.

Meyer, Joyce. *Overcoming Every Problem*. New York: FaithWords, 2023.

"Postpartum Depression: Causes, Risks and Treatment: UPMC Central PA." *UPMC*. www.upmc.com/services/south-central-pa/women/services/ pregnancy-childbirth/new-moms/postpartum-depression/risks-treat- ment. Accessed August 29, 2024.

Schwenk, Ruth. *The Better Mom Devotional*. Grand Rapids: Zondervan, 2018.

Also by Alexandra Jensen

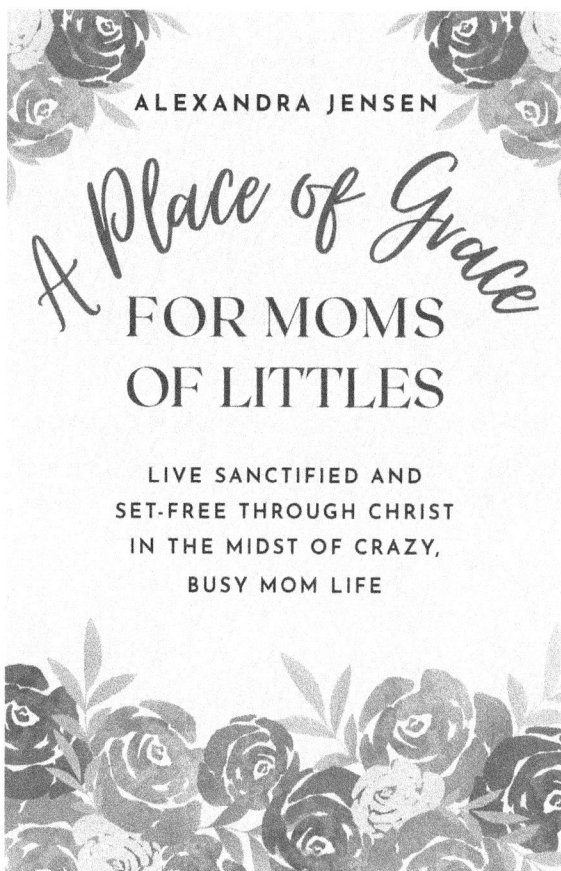

ALEXANDRA JENSEN

A Place of Grace

FOR MOMS
OF LITTLES

LIVE SANCTIFIED AND
SET-FREE THROUGH CHRIST
IN THE MIDST OF CRAZY,
BUSY MOM LIFE

FINDING A HAPPY Home

A JOURNEY OF FAITH AND REDEMPTION

JILL VAN OPSTAL-POPA

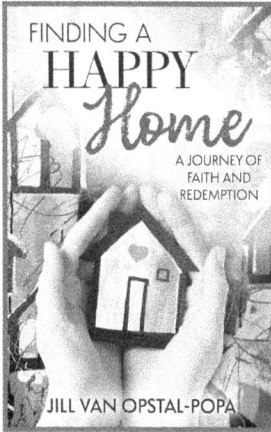

Growing up in small-town Ohio, Jill van Opstal-Popa never dreamed she would be making her home among the orphaned children of Brazil. But when she and her husband set out to be missionaries, they found themselves building a home for the children who had no home. In *Finding a Happy Home: A Journey of Faith and Redemption*, from the heart of a mother to many comes the stories of the people of Brazil. Your heart will be pulled to the stories of each child whose story is unique but also like so many others.

Take some deep breaths with Bonica Brown, who has found what her soul has been thirsting for in God's Word and in the gift of His roses and honeysuckle. With examples of her own imperfect life, Bonica points the reader to Scripture to find beauty in the mess of kissing boo-boos, cleaning up a sick child, and trying to look like a family who has it altogether for Sunday morning church. If you have ever needed a friend to walk through the ups and downs of motherhood with you, Bonica is waiting for you to introduce you to her very Best Friend, Jesus Christ.

Finding God in the Midst of an Ordinary Life

Roses & HONEYSUCKLE

BONICA BROWN

FULLNESS OF JOY

ONE HUNDRED DEVOTIONS TO BRING YOU INTO GOD'S PRESENCE

ELIZABETH RICE HANDFORD

Throughout her years serving alongside her husband, who pastored Southside Baptist Church (now Fellowship Greenville) in Greenville, South Carolina, for over thirty years, Elizabeth Rice Handford has had the opportunity to touch many lives with her daily devotionals. In her new devotional, *Fullness of Joy*, take a dive into one hundred of Libby's devotionals, compiled from a look back through her writings and life experiences.